A Benevolent
Virus

A Benevolent Virus

Virus

Frances O'Brien

BOOKS

Winchester, UK
Washington, USA

First published by O-Books, 2010

O Books is an imprint of John Hunt Publishing Ltd., The Bothy, Deershot Lodge, Park Lane, Ropley, Hants, SO24 0BE, UK
office1@o-books.net
www.o-books.com

For distributor details and how to order please visit the 'Ordering' section on our website.

Text copyright Frances O'Brien 2009

ISBN: 978 1 84694 432 1

A CIP catalogue record for this book is available from the British Library.

Design: Stuart Davies

Printed in the UK by CPI Antony Rowe
Printed in the USA by Offset Paperback Mfrs, Inc

We operate a distinctive and ethical publishing philosophy in all areas of its business, from its global network of authors to production and worldwide distribution.

For Jeff, Conor and Orla

The true nature of things loves to hide itself.

Heraclitus, 500 BC

Chapter 1

Nobody's life is ever really saved. The best anyone can ever hope to do is to postpone the inevitable.

Ann Richards had lobbed that particular idea into otherwise dull dinner party conversations on more than one occasion. It was not that she was a particularly philosophical woman. But she was a pragmatic woman with a low boredom threshold.

If pressed, Ann would have argued that death had become a dirty word; the price people paid for bad habits, bad diets or the simple bad luck of being in the wrong place at the wrong time. An obsession with health and fitness had seduced otherwise sensible people into the comforting notion that death was some sort of bullet that they could dodge if they simply tried harder and ate less.

Ann knew that we all have to go sometime, but equally she saw no merit in any prolonged contemplation of oblivion. She was, after all, only 47 years old. The odds were clearly stacked in her favour.

There was nothing in that particular Monday morning to suggest anything out of the ordinary was about to happen.

True, Ann was feeling sluggish, but she was pretty sure that the rest of the country was probably feeling much the same way as everyone returned to work after the Thanksgiving holiday weekend. She'd read somewhere that turkey had a sedative effect. Burgundy had certainly consumed some of her brain cells over Thanksgiving.

Lately she had noticed that her body was slower to recover from any over-indulgence. Once again she knew that she would have reason to be grateful for the fact that she had never gotten around to installing a weighing scales in the bathroom of their weekend holiday home. There would be plenty of opportunity for abstinence and exercise once she returned to the city.

Consciousness wouldn't really kick in until she'd had her first cup of coffee. But somehow the sheer force of will that would be required of her to part company with the duvet seemed unobtainable in the sleepy haze that always followed the shrieking of her alarm clock. The seductiveness of half-remembered dreams threatened to beckon her back to sleep. She fought this threat by sending forth her left hand to grope for the remote control on her nightstand. One expert click filled her bedroom with the sounds of the morning news. Stories of share prices, wars and weather alerts could always be relied upon to get her brain in gear. She turned over and lay on her back, letting the impossibly perky newscaster's voice float over her, as she focused on opening her eyes.

Stephen had been gone for hours. He had left before first light, buzzing with the kind of excitement that always shot through him just before one of his takeovers. Their relationship could so easily have faltered in the early days if Stephen's bafflement at Ann's struggle with mornings had been mistaken for laziness. But there has been too much high-achieving evidence to the contrary, and he had learned to live with this anomaly. Like all married couples they had each learned to make compromises.

Likewise, it had simply not occurred to her to be bothered by the fact that Stephen had spent much of the holiday weekend in his study. Instead, she had used her journalistic skills to prod him with just the right kind of questions about his latest venture each time he had emerged, for the simple pleasure of sharing in his excitement.

Ann was not a needy woman. What could she possibly need when she had the tranquillity of their place in the Hamptons? Trips to their beach-side home were the perfect antidote to the frantic pace of their city existence.

Here she swapped her high heels for Crocs. Grooming was kept to an absolute minimum, and she found to her delight that this low-maintenance, dressed-down look was her passport to anonymity whenever she had need to leave the house.

For the most part she had spent the weekend walking alone through the sand dunes or catching up on her reading in some quiet, warm corner in their huge, wind-swept home.

It had been a wonderful weekend; if anything, her happiness had been heightened by the feeling that she was in some way playing hooky. She had once again escaped the tyranny of a full family Thanksgiving. The fact that her Mom had opted to spend the holiday with her brother's family on the west coast had certainly given her reason to give thanks. What were her Mom's plans for Christmas?

That dark thought drove her to throw off the duvet. As she stumbled into the bathroom she knew that the image that she presented to the mirror would have shocked her viewers. Her blonde hair had a serious case of bed-head. It was probably best not to dwell too long on the fact that mornings were clearly not kind to her face. This was the time of day when all of her resistance to cosmetic surgery was at its weakest. Principles didn't count for much when faced with her own scary reflection first thing in the morning. It was something to remember next time she was presented with a surgically-enhanced clone who expected to be taken seriously in an interview situation. Maybe all of those poor, demented celebrities had been accosted by some cosmetic surgeon who prowled the bathrooms of the rich and famous at an ungodly hour of the morning, offering promises of long-lost youth, and striking before they had even had a cup of coffee to restore their ability to think clearly. Yeah, sure. That would explain everything.

She quickly sought salvation in the warm waters of the shower. That was better. In only a few hours she would morph into the face of the network's highest-rated news magazine show. With some expert hair and make-up, not to mention some careful lighting, she would soon be the Ann Richards known to millions across America.

Today she would definitely schedule some time with Katherine. Ever since Katherine had become executive producer of the show, Ann had been lumbered with more than her fair share of soft, emotional interview pieces that usually ended in tears. Despite winning two Emmys, Ann now spent much of her time acting as public confessor to errant politicians and comforter to survivors of catastrophes.

The briefing notes for today's planned interview with Congressman Reiner had confirmed Ann's suspicion that she and Katherine needed to have a serious conversation. Sure, there was public interest in a Congressman who decided to come out of the closet, but it was hardly a serious news item. There was nothing to suggest that the man had been anything other than honest and hardworking in his political life. Ann was uncomfortable about grilling the man over the peculiarities of his private life. It was less a news item than a thinly-veiled piece of gossip.

Ann's anger quickly got her back into work mode. She ignored the jeans and leisurewear in her dressing room and reached for a black Donna Karan dress. That was better.

Anita, her housekeeper, had arranged the morning papers in the breakfast room, and though Ann always skipped breakfast, she appreciated the fact that Anita tried to coax her with an offer of scrambled eggs. In the end Anita delivered Ann's carafe of coffee with a plate of sliced fruit, although both women knew that the fruit would remain untouched.

There was no better smell in the world than the particular combination of fresh coffee and morning newspapers. Even after five years, this was the time of day when Ann most craved a cigarette. But instead she charged into the papers, knowing that her cell phone would soon interrupt this morning bliss.

Ann had wanted to avoid the early-morning traffic on the Long Island Expressway, so she had asked the studio to send a car mid-morning. The sheer indulgence of her late departure gave her precious extra moments to read some of her favorite columnists without disruption.

Her assistant was the first to call, with changes to the week's schedule. The remainder of her morning at home was taken up with some follow-up questions for an interview that was scheduled to run in the most popular women's magazine in the US.

The reporter (my God, did that mean that the perky clothes-horse who had sucked up two hours of her time last week had an actual degree in journalism?) wanted to know if Ann had any diet tips to share with her readers. Ann suppressed the urge to recommend that her readers get a life, and instead regurgitated the advice that her trainer gave to her on a weekly basis. She smiled as she stressed the importance of breakfast; she even claimed a taste for oatmeal.

How exactly had Ann managed to become a poster-girl for the middle-aged women of America? She knew that once she reached the office she would have to approve the cover shot that they planned to accompany her interview piece. And given that at least a dozen people had participated in that shoot in a Manhattan loft (that was another two hours of her life that she would never have back!), she knew that she would look nothing like the woman who had stared back at her in the bathroom this morning. When exactly had journalists become celebrities and cover girls?

Ann's role models had been made of tougher stuff. Her heroes had been Woodward and Bernstein. She had wanted to be a truth teller; she had wanted to uncover great political and corporate conspiracies.

Looking back, she had been pretty naïve. Maybe America no longer had the stomach for news that challenged them to look outside of their comfort zone? Or maybe she'd just gotten lazy.

Whatever it was, Ann knew that it was time to shake things up. She had some serious ideas, and she and her producer needed to have a very frank discussion. Things would be different in the New Year, she would make sure of it.

She planned to use the car journey to produce the first draft of her weekly column. Driving was not only a waste of time, but she had lived in New York long enough to know that it was not one of her core competencies. The drivers used by the studio were all reliable, ex-military guys and they were all regularly drug tested.

Ann knew she was in safe hands as she slid into the back of the limo. As the car swept through some of the wealthiest streets in Long Island, Ann was thinking only of her column. By the time her car reached the highway, Ann had opened her laptop computer and was busy writing about the most recent and damning survey of standards in inner-city schools. She wondered if she could use the piece as the basis for a show. Surely the failing education of the nation's poorest children was more important than the sex lives of the Washington elite?

Even if Ann had looked out of her window, she would have had little notice of the accident that was to come. Reports later claimed that the Porsche 911 was travelling at over 90 miles per hour when its rear left tyre had a blow out. It had spun out of the driver's control by the time it ran into the path of Ann's limo. The Porsche hit the left rear side of the limo with such force that it was sent into a tailspin that only ended when the limo reached the very edge of the highway.

It was there that the limo was hit by a pickup truck. The force of the second impact caused the limo to roll over twice before it came to rest on its roof.

Time takes on different properties in the course of a road traffic accident. From Ann's perspective everything appeared to happen in a grotesque slow motion. The noise was beyond anything that could be produced by special effects. That shattering sound of high speed metal on metal was Ann's first sign that she was in danger. But in that split-second instant of the crash, she was powerless to act.

The contents of the limousine exploded in all directions. Her computer and purse suddenly became missiles. The force of the seat belt against her chest forced the air from her lungs.

There was absolute chaos, and surprisingly, no time to feel scared. By the time the crumpled limo came to a halt, Ann's broken body was suspended, upside down, held there by her seatbelt in the midst of twisted metal and broken glass. And somewhere in the wreckage, her cell phone was ringing.

The human body often reacts to such catastrophic events by shutting down. Ann must have passed out for a short time, because when she regained consciousness the ringing of her cell phone had been replaced by the sound of sirens approaching. A car's horn was honking somewhere. And was that country music she could hear?

She tried to open her eyes, but there was too much blood. The first tide of pain and panic swept over her. Everything hurt. It even hurt to breathe. Maybe she should just try to sleep. There was nothing she could do.

For the first time in her life Ann Richards surrendered to her fate.

She had expected to sleep. But somehow she found herself standing outside the wreckage of the limo. Fear and pain had suddenly been replaced by a feeling of peace. Although Ann had built a career on her intense curiosity, she was only vaguely interested to notice that she appeared to be able to move around the scene of the accident at will. She sensed that she was floating. Everything was beginning to make perfect sense.

Her attention was moved to the red Ford pickup truck that had landed on its side far behind the limo. She heard a woman's crying.

Moving closer, she watched as a thirty-something woman pulled herself up through the truck's window. She was clearly cradling something in her arms. Despite the cuts to her face and arms, the woman's attention was devoted to this precious cargo. Was it a baby? As the woman staggered to the side of the highway Ann saw that the woman was holding a small dog. The lifeless creature was a bloody mass of brown and black fur. Clearly shaking now, the woman fell to the ground and held her dog to her chest as she started to rock. She cried and repeated the name, 'Archie' at a whisper as she began to take in the scene of devastation that surrounded her.

Ann wanted to reassure the woman. But the woman was clearly in too much shock to even notice Ann's existence. The arrival of a paramedic to the woman's side freed Ann to further survey the damage.

Oddly, the attention of the rescue services appeared to be centred around the limo. Ann tried to reassure the fire crew and the waiting paramedics that she was fine, in fact, she had never felt better, but they were too busy to hear her. Looking closer, Ann saw that there was someone trapped in the back of the limo. The woman was clearly in bad shape. Ann did not know that a human body could lose that much blood and survive.

'Jesus, it's Ann Richards,' said the young paramedic who was first to reach the woman's body, 'and I'm not picking up a pulse.'

Was Ann dead?

Could death really feel this good?

Ann seemed to move away from the scene of the accident as she considered this possibility.

She wanted everyone to know that there was no need to worry. A feeling of ecstasy overwhelmed her. This was good. No, this was beyond good. This was great.

It was then that Ann first noticed the bright light that was shining behind her right shoulder. Did light have feeling? It was time to move on, and Ann felt as if she knew where she was going.

Chapter 2

Daniel was too busy with his new camera to notice that his subject was squirming in his chair.

Even if he had noticed Jake Matthews' obvious discomfort, it is unlikely that Daniel would have known how to put the man at ease. The fact was, Daniel was hardly comfortable in his new role as interviewer. Plus, the HD camcorder that he planned to use was less than the size of the palm of his hand, and impressive though that was, it meant that the controls were difficult to operate with his thick fingers.

Jake pulled at his tie as Daniel finally clicked the camcorder into the tripod. As Daniel took his seat opposite Jake, out of shot, he wondered where to begin.

For the first time that day he felt a wave of anxiety. The two men were strangers. Neither man looked like the kind of guy who made a habit of talking about their feelings. Jake's huge frame had been squeezed into a suit that, Daniel guessed, was reserved almost exclusively for family weddings and funerals.

Daniel, though dressed-down in jeans and a T-shirt, still looked every inch the military man. It wasn't just the precisely cropped hair that gave him away. Somehow, his years in the Marines had changed his posture. He moved with a certainty and confidence that suggested he could handle any threat.

'You can just forget about the camera,' said Daniel as he glanced down at his notes.

Jake took another sip of water and looked directly into Daniel's eyes.

'Why don't you just begin by telling your story?' Daniel asked.

'My story,' said Jake, with a smile, 'it's not something I exactly talk about a whole lot, you know? Of course, I told my wife Suzy. She knows everything about it. But it was different back then.

9

Suicide was not what you might call a topic for conversation. Not that anyone ever came out and asked me if that's what I planned to do that night, you know? Commit suicide? When people did talk about it, they talked about my accident. As if driving a car into a tree at 70 miles per hour was ever an accident...'

He smiled. 'Still, I'm getting ahead of myself, I suppose. You'll want to know what made a seventeen-year-old boy want to do that, right?'

Jake paused, clearly lost in his memories.

'Mama died in 1973. It was the breast cancer that took her. She wasted away before our very eyes. Papa took it real hard. Course, he'd always been a drinker. But when Mama was alive, he mostly drank beer. After she died, he turned to whiskey.

'To begin with, I think he drank to help him sleep. I'd hear him wandering round the house late at night and in the morning I'd come downstairs and find the bottle. Soon he'd hit the whiskey as soon as he got home from the factory in the afternoon.

'It was just the two of us by then. My brother David had gone into the army. I think he joined up just to get as far away from that house as he could. And I didn't blame him for that – I had big plans of my own. Hard to believe, I know,' he said, patting his belly, 'but I was a real jock back then. High school coach reckoned I was a sure thing for a sports scholarship.

'In my mind, I had my whole future planned out, you know? I was going to college to be a big football star. I could practically taste it. That dream kept me going. It was the reason I got up in the morning and it was the reason I worked harder than any other boy on the field.

'About a month before the college scouts were due in town something terrible happened. Another player came crashing into me during a high school league game. I felt him hit the side of my knee and then I felt this pop, you know? My knee blew up to the size of a melon. It hurt like hell. Turns out that popping was the ligament in the centre of my knee being torn. Doc said it was the worst he'd ever seen. And nothing I did seemed to help. My knee felt loose. In fact it still feels loose sometimes. And just that one pop, that one tackle, was enough to put an end to my college dreams forever.

'Course, it took some time for me to accept that fact. But one day I just couldn't get my butt out of bed. There didn't seem to be a point to anything. Papa didn't even realize that I hadn't gone to school, he just went to work, and I was left alone at home to face the blackest day of my life.

'All that grief of losing my Mama, of losing my chance of going to college and of having that great football career – well, it hit me all at once. Everything seemed hopeless. I'd always worked hard and done my best, but suddenly it seemed pretty damned clear to me that my best was nowhere near good enough. So what was the point?

'I don't know that I consciously wanted to kill myself when I left the house that afternoon. I really just wanted to stop all of the pain because it was more than I could bear. And I knew that I had to be gone before Papa got back from work.

'So I took the key to the beaten up old Lincoln that Papa and I had been working on before Mama died and I hoped it had some gas. When the ignition fired it was kind of exciting, but pretty soon it hurt to remember all those good memories of fixing up that car with my Dad.

'As I started to drive I felt so angry with him for giving up on me. Hating him was the only feeling that was bigger than my despair that day. The madder I got, the faster I drove. Pretty soon I was out of town and the sky was getting darker. My foot was to the floor and I started to have trouble controlling that old car, when suddenly, I wondered why I was even bothering to try. I saw a big oak tree at a bend that was maybe 60 feet ahead and I didn't even try to make the corner.'

Jake, looking wide-eyed stopped for a sip of water.

'What happened next?' asked Daniel.

'Well, what do you think?' said Jake. 'That car hit that tree just like I'd planned – Pow! The noise was tremendous. Course the Lincoln didn't have any seatbelts, not that I would have been wearing one, you understand. My body was thrown from the wreckage. The impact was enough to kill anyone. So that should have been that...'

There was a pause.

'Except of course, nothing happened the way I'd imagined. I found myself in a kind of darkness. I didn't have a body exactly, but I was still me, you know? And even though I couldn't see anything or anyone else there, I knew that I was not alone. It felt like there were others there who really understood my pain, and all they wanted to do was to comfort me. Seems like I was there for quite some time before I noticed the light...

'It was a tiny speck at first. But once I gave it my attention, I began to move towards it. The sensation of speed and my motion toward this amazing light made it seem like I was in some kind of tunnel.

'When I finally broke through into that light it was like experiencing the best feeling you have ever had in this world and multiplying it times a million. It was like scoring a million touchdowns at a Super Bowl game – though really it was more than that.

'I knew my Mama was there even before I saw her. And when I did look at her, she looked better than I had ever seen her before in my life. There was no trace of her illness. None. She spoke into my mind, not with words, but with her thoughts. And she told me that this was not my time.

'Another spirit, or being, that was next to my Mama gently told me I would have to leave. As I tried to argue that I wanted to stay, I felt myself being reminded of the fact that I had agreed to my life. I remembered that my soul had chosen to experience my life just exactly as it was, and that I could not go home to that beautiful place, until I had fulfilled my purpose.

'And just in that moment I knew what that purpose was...

Course I couldn't remember the details of what that purpose was once I got back here – no matter how I tried.

'They knew I was disappointed to have to leave. I knew they wanted to console me before I came back. And maybe that's why I was allowed to remember their last words to me.

'They told me life would be simple if I remembered that all I really had to do was to love. With that, I felt myself being sucked back into my body. The last thing I remember about that whole experience was thinking that I would never be able to squeeze back into the body that was lying next to that oak tree.

'Next thing I knew, I was waking up in hospital. The pain was unbearable, but I do recall it was the first time I'd seen Papa sober in a long, long time.'

Daniel did not interrupt the silence that followed Jake's disclosure. Jake took a deep breath and smiled; clearly relieved to have told his story.

'Course, Papa didn't exactly encourage me to talk when I told him I'd seen Mama. Pretty soon I learned to keep the whole thing to myself.'

'How did the experience change you?' asked Daniel.

'It changed everything about me,' said Jake, 'it changed the way I thought about the world. For a time it bothered me. I wondered why such a mind-blowing thing had happened to me, I mean, I was no-one special.

'But you can't be loved like that and not change. I knew I was loved, even when I had failed, even when I did not love myself. And for reasons that I may never fathom, I knew, just knew that my life had purpose, even though that life was never going to be the life that I had dreamed about before. That's pretty powerful.'

'Are you a religious person?' asked Daniel. 'Do you go to church?'

'You'd really think I would go to church now, wouldn't you?' Jake answered. 'But the fact is I don't. When I think about church, I think about lots of rules and lots of judgements, you know? And I know the truth is a lot simpler than that.

'So I don't go to church, but that's not to say I don't pray. Sometimes I feel my whole life is a prayer. Not a prayer like you'd say in church, but a prayer of loving and being loved. I give a lot of love to the people in my life, but I get a whole lot of love back in return. Why wouldn't I thank God for that?'

'Do you believe in life after death?' asked Daniel finally.

'I don't believe,' said Jake with a huge chuckle. 'I know.'

Frances O'Brien

Chapter 3

All hospitals have a medical smell. Ann didn't even need to open
her eyes to know that she was lying in a hospital bed. At first she
was only aware of that peculiar antiseptic odour. Then she
realized she could hear sounds. There was a soothing rhythmic
beeping somewhere nearby. At times she could hear footsteps
and occasionally even voices, but like the blurred outline of some
distant shore, she could not understand a thing that she heard,
although she knew that she was not on her own.

It was the pain that forced her back into consciousness. Her
chest hurt, and each breath she took seemed to exacerbate a
feeling of sharp discomfort. The pain forced her to shift slightly
in the bed, but that small movement seemed to drive a knife into
her hips. She flinched and forced her eyes to open slightly.

There was a window. The light that flooded into the room
blinded Ann for that first moment. She shifted her gaze to the
flowers. The bright colours of the floral arrangements that filled
the room helped her to regain some focus. Soon the wild blend
of pinks, greens, whites and reds transformed into individually
identifiable flowers and ferns.

The sound of a commercial break alerted her to the fact that
there was a television in the room. Her first painful experience of
movement made her reluctant to move her head to see if there
was anyone watching the television. She took several breaths
before she shifted her head slightly to see who, if anyone, was
there with her.

At first sight, her Mom almost looked comical. She had clearly
fallen asleep in the chair that she had pulled directly in front of
the TV and the result would have mortified the normally elegant
Moira Richards. With her mouth opened wide and her glasses
perched perilously at the end of her nose, she looked every one

of her 72 years of age.

For the first time in a long time, Ann felt a wave of love and compassion for her mother.

'Mom,' whispered Ann, but her mother did not stir.

Ann's throat had never felt so dry.

'Mom, Mom,' said Ann, her cry more urgent now.

Miraculously, her Mom heard. Although she was startled out of her nap, she moved quickly towards her daughter. She hit the call button before she grabbed Ann's hand.

'That's my girl Ann,' she said, 'I knew you'd wake up, I just knew it.'

Ann had not seen her mother cry since her Dad's funeral fourteen years before, but Moira Richards made no attempt to hide her tears from the medical personnel who now raced into Ann's room. Her gaze never left her daughter.

'Water,' whispered Ann to the nurse who was adjusting her bed so that Ann now had a clearer view of her room.

A doctor of about Ann's age surveyed Ann carefully before speaking.

'My name is Doctor Walker. You're in the hospital. You were brought to us five days ago, after your car was involved in a collision. Do you remember the crash?'

Ann nodded gently, careful not to move any more than was necessary. She was grateful to see the nurse return to the room with some iced water and a straw. That first sip of water was delicious; it encouraged her to attempt to speak once more.

'Everything hurts,' she said hoarsely.

'We'll do something about that, don't you worry,' said the doctor. 'Ann you arrived here with multiple injuries. We had to perform surgery on your heart. Your aorta was torn and there was air around your lungs, so Doctor Steinberg performed a procedure called a pericardial window and then repaired your aorta. He then discovered some lacerations to your spleen and liver. You also have fractures to your hips, ribs and collarbone.

These are serious injuries Ann. So we have kept you sedated. You lost a lot of blood. Your condition is stable, so please let us take care of you. We'll get your pain under control. Do you understand?'

'Yes,' said Ann as she tried to make some sense of her situation.

Doctor Walker tracked the movement of her eyes as her gaze followed the stick that he paraded about six inches from her face.

'I just need to ask you some simple questions now,' said the doctor.

'Can you tell me your full name?'

'Ann Richards.'

And what month is this, Ann?'

'November, December? I'm not sure'

The Doctor nodded. 'And what's your date of birth, Ann?'

'May 10th 1960.'

Obviously happy with her responses, Doctor Walker took Ann's chart and consulted with the nurses, allowing Ann's Mom to resume her position beside Ann's bed.

Moira Richards held her daughter's hand with a fierce maternal protection that she was surprised to find that she still possessed.

'I've called Stephen,' she said. 'He had to go the city. He'll be so disappointed to have missed this. He wanted to be here when you woke. But he'll be here soon.'

'It was so beautiful Mom,' said Ann.

Moira looked confused but compassionate. 'What was so beautiful, darling?' she asked.

'Everything... everything. You'll see.'

A nurse delivered a welcome shot for the pain while Moira smoothed her daughter's blonde hair.

'I saw Daddy,' said Ann

'That's nice dear,' said Moira. 'I'm glad that cocktail of

medication has given you such pretty dreams. You deserve pretty dreams.'

Ann tried to raise her head from the pillow.

'And Lauren,' said Ann.

Moira Richards froze.

'Daddy was there, and Lauren was with him. Why did you never tell me I had a sister?'

Chapter 4

Daniel hesitated before beginning his questioning. There was something so open and so very vulnerable in the face of Sarah Jenkins that he felt that his camera was somehow an intruder. Sarah had done everything to make him feel at ease as soon as he had arrived at the door of her St Augustine home half an hour earlier. She was clearly a willing subject. But Daniel had never before met anyone who was blind.

The tactile nature of Sarah's welcome had left him feeling a little off balance. After the long car journey to the Florida holiday town, Daniel had been unprepared for her warm hug and for the careful examination that her fingers had made of his face and hair.

Now that they were both seated in her small, bright kitchen, Daniel felt a shot of something close to guilt before he began the interview.

Although she had worn a neatly-pressed white shirt and blue skirt for the occasion, Daniel saw that her face was free of any make-up. Despite the fact that there was nothing to camouflage the lines and blemishes of her 58 years, Sarah Jenkins was clearly happy in her own skin.

She smiled broadly with excitement; keen to share her story.

Daniel began with the most obvious question. 'Sarah, have you been blind from birth?'

'Yes I have,' Sarah replied, still smiling. 'I was born six weeks premature back in 1950 and I'm one of the many babies who were left blinded by a new type of air-lock incubator that they had just invented back then. Those incubators delivered too much oxygen.

'It took some time for scientists to realize that they were destroying our optic nerves with those things. It was too late for me and plenty more like me by the time they figured out their mistake. So I've always been blind.'

Sarah shrugged resignedly, but the smile never left her face.

'Can you tell me what happened to you on July 4th 1959?' asked Daniel.

'Well, first you'd have to understand the sort of kid I was back then,' said Sarah. ' I was the youngest of five kids. There was only a year or two between each of us. I had two sisters and two brothers. My parents never fussed over me or made me feel like there were things that I couldn't do. I did everything my brothers and sisters did. Playing outdoors so much, I got to know my way around the neighbourhood real well, though I probably fell over more often than the other kids did.

'Like all little sisters, I guess I could be pretty annoying, and on that July 4th I was fit to burst with excitement. There was a big fireworks display planned for later on that evening and I simply could not wait for the party.

'I must have got under my Mom's feet one time too many, because she told my sister Pam to go play with me in the yard. Pam was not impressed to be left babysitting me on that hot afternoon. But then what thirteen-year-old girl wants to be lumbered with an over-excited nine-year-old? She would not let me braid her hair and she refused to bring her new transistor radio outside. When I started teasing her about Tommy Sullivan, a new kid in the neighbourhood, she decided she'd had enough of me. She told me to get lost and she went back indoors.

'And that would have been that. That should have been that, except I got an idea in my head. I remembered that our neighbours were out of town for the holiday, and unlike us, they had a pool.

'None of us was allowed to swim without permission or supervision. I knew what I was doing was wrong. When I moved the wobbly fence panel that separated our yards I just hoped that nobody would spot me.

'I decided that all I would do was cool my feet down in the

water; I wasn't wearing a swimsuit and I didn't want to get busted. Things went wrong as I was unbuckling my right sandal. I couldn't get that thing off quickly enough, and when I yanked it off, I lost my balance. My head hit the tile that bordered the pool so hard that I lost consciousness and fell into the water.

'And that's when all the weirdness began.

'My first awareness was of a popping sound. I think that's when I left my body. You'd think I would have been scared, but I wasn't, at least not until I realized that I could see...

'My world until then had been all about touch, taste, smell and sound. So when people spoke about colors, I never knew what they meant. It was like they were speaking a language that I just didn't understand. My brothers and sisters tried to explain colors to me lots of times. So when I wriggled my toes in the grass, I knew that was green. And when I felt the hot sun on my face, I knew that was white. I was told that black was the opposite of white, so I understood black to be cold. The soft cashmere sweater that Pam had got for her thirteenth birthday was pink. You see what I mean?

'I understand,' said Daniel.

'So, as I floated above my body and out of the pool I was less freaked out about leaving my body than I was about trying to make sense of the things that I was seeing for the first time.

'The thing that hit me first was the way the sky looked. That was something my brothers and sisters had never managed to get through to me; the blueness of the sky. I mean it wasn't as though I would feel the sky whenever they tried to explain. So for a while I looked only at the sky so that I could get my first experience of blue. And that gave me a huge sense of peace.

'Suddenly everything felt amazing. There was a rightness to everything that I was experiencing. I felt that somehow I was a part of everything.

'If Pam hadn't come running into the yard just at that moment, I think I would have continued floating. Who knows where I would have gone? I heard Pam scream for Mom before I realized she was standing next to the pool.

' It was the first time that I had ever seen her, and I remember noticing that her hair was the same shade of brightness as the roses that were blooming in our yard. Her dress was a pattern of lines of lots of different colors. She dived into the pool and grabbed me to the surface.

'I never did get a good look at my face. When Pam managed to finally pull me to the side of the pool, I was face down. But I did notice that my dress was the exact same color as my sandals, and the pattern was filled with lots of bright tiny circles. It was nice, but I remember thinking how I preferred Pam's dress.

'I was not at all concerned about what was going on. I felt perfectly fine.

'Hearing Mom's scream changed things. She sounded like a wild, injured animal. I was still face-down when she pulled me onto her lap. And she started hitting my back, like her life depended upon it. Water poured out of my mouth. And then she started shaking me real hard.

'She said "Sarah Louise Anderson, you are not dying on me today. Do you hear me? You are not dying on me today."

'I swear I could feel the power of her emotions. It occurred to me that I could return to my body if I wanted to. And that's exactly what I did, but not before noticing that my Mom's eyes were the same bright colour as the sky.

'I coughed all the way to the hospital. Mom never let me out of her arms as one of our neighbors, Mrs Burns drove us there. They kept me in for observation. But I was fine. I guess I had no-one to blame but myself for missing out on that party…

'Did you ever talk to your family about what happened to you that day?' asked Daniel.

'Mom would get mad if I ever tried to talk about it, so I never got to tell her. But I did tell Pam. And I know Pam believed me. She confirmed for me that the dress and sandals that I wore that day were red. And that her blonde hair was the same shade as the flowers in our rosebush. She also told me that Mom's eyes were blue, just like the sky.'

Sarah paused for a moment, deep in thought.

'But I didn't need that confirmation, not for one moment. I was always clear in my own mind about what happened that day. I know my spirit left my body and I know I saw everything that happened from that point on; colors, faces, everything.'

'How did the experience change you?' asked Daniel.

'Knowing that I had a soul and knowing how good that felt, made me very curious about God,' said Sarah. 'I nagged Mom into taking me to church. There was a feeling that I wanted to visit God's house. Mom took me a few times, but she was not at all keen. So I took to praying privately in my own room. I even kept a set of rosary beads that a neighbour had given me and put then on my nightstand so that I could feel a little closer to God.'

'How about now?' Asked Daniel 'Do you still pray or go to church?'

Sarah laughed.

'These days my church going is strictly limited to weddings and funerals. I did experiment a little in my twenties; I visited lots of churches, but I could never really find a fit. No church ever did make me feel as right and as happy as I did when I had my brush with death.

'As for praying, well I pray if by prayer you mean talking to God. We talk every day.

'You know, you asked me how this changed me and the best way I can think to explain it is this; I no longer believe that I am a body with a soul, now I know that I am, in fact, a soul experiencing a body. And that makes a world of a difference to how I think about my time here on this earth.'

Chapter 5

Stephen had always viewed doctors as being little more than mechanics. He attended medical screenings and checkups in much the same way as he made sure his cars were regularly serviced. The time that he invested with his trainer was non-negotiable, and the dividends were clear to see; at almost 55, he was in the best shape of his life. He took responsibility for his body and it was his expectation that doctors would hold up their end of the bargain and fix him should that need ever arise.

So he had struggled to hide his frustration when Ann's doctor had been less than clear on when she could be expected to make a complete recovery.

Dr Steinberg had an excellent reputation. In fact, it was his reputation that had been the deciding factor when Stephen had elected not to move Ann to another facility shortly after the accident. Now, almost three weeks after the crash, Stephen had cause to regret that decision. Clearly the shock of almost losing his wife had compromised his decision-making and Stephen was beginning to realize that negotiations with the medical profession were never as straightforward as his business dealings.

'Your wife is making a remarkable recovery,' said Dr Steinberg.

The man practically oozed empathy. Stephen had to force himself not to squirm in his chair. He had requested this meeting in the doctor's office so that he could speak freely with the man, but there was something deeply maddening and equally disarming in negotiating with someone who dealt in the currency of life and death. The professional air of compassion almost made it impossible for Stephen to express himself with the force that he needed to make his point.

'It's not at all unusual to feel anxious about returning home with a loved one when they are not fully healed. But I can assure you that your wife is making excellent progress, and we believe that with the right support in place, she can return home this Friday. She has recovered well from surgery. The physiotherapists assure me that she is a model patient. What she needs now is time and rest. She will heal better at home.'

Was the doctor trying to patronize him? Stephen decided it was time to cut through this touchy-feely talk of healing. He did nothing to hide his anger. It was time to make the doctor understand him.

'What about my wife's brain injuries?' he exploded. 'Will they be healed by Friday?'

Dr Steinberg took a deep breath before replying.

'I understand your concern Stephen,' he replied. 'Your wife has suffered a serious trauma. But our psychological evaluation shows that her cognitive ability has not been impaired. All of our tests show that Ann has no permanent brain damage.'

'So let me get this straight,' said Stephen, 'there is no physical reason that could explain why my wife is claiming to have taken a day trip to heaven with her dead Dad and sister? That's a benchmark of the cognitive abilities that you and your staff here expect to see in patients before they're discharged?'

Dr Steinberg contorted his face into a practiced expression of concern, giving yet another display of his unending professional empathy.

'Recovery from traumatic incidents can sometimes involve a change in personality,' he said. 'I cannot tell you with any degree of certainty if such a change is permanent or not. There isn't a doctor in any facility who could give you an accurate answer to that question at this time. I fully appreciate how frustrating this is for you, but what your wife needs now is time to heal. You'll both feel better when she goes home.'

Stephen leaned forward, placing his clenched fists on the doctor's antique desk.

'With respect Doctor, you cannot tell me with any degree of certainty how I will feel if this situation continues,' he said. 'The woman I married isn't some religious nut; she's a logical, intelligent woman. How can you tell me that she hasn't been brain damaged when all of the evidence points to the contrary?

'When my wife got into that car she was at the top of her game. She's built her entire career on sharp thinking and clear communication. That pile-up has left her claiming to have had some sort of mystical experience. She has clearly been damaged. And with respect Dr Steinberg, I can only conclude that you are missing something.'

Dr Steinberg remained remarkably unflustered.

'This is not as uncommon as you may think,' said the doctor. 'I've come across cases like your wife's before; often when there has been no brain trauma of any kind.

'There is no simple scientific explanation for what Ann is going through. Coming face to face with your own mortality can change a person.'

He paused to gauge Stephen's response, and then continued.

'Clearly your wife currently believes that she experienced a spiritual encounter of some kind in the aftermath of her accident. And if that is a source of comfort to her at this time, I cannot see how it can harm her.

'Personally, my training would lead me to a different interpretation of her experience. Science is my religion. How about you Stephen? Do you believe in God?'

'I believe in what I can see,' said Stephen.

Dr Steinberg nodded in agreement.

'We know that there is an area in the right temporal lobe that can sometimes cause these seemingly very real religious experiences. Massive injuries can cause the body to flood with endorphins that sometimes produce a similar effect to a drug trip – it's the brain's way of coping with huge shock and pain... The effect can be so powerful that patients sometimes actually believe that they are outside of their bodies. Even test pilots who experience hypoxia and a decreased flow of oxygen to the brain have reported similar stories of seemingly inexplicable phenomena.

'There are many complex mechanisms available to the brain in time of trauma. None of them are in themselves evidence of any long-term damage.

'The shock of a catastrophic accident can cause even the sharpest of minds to seek refuge in spiritual experiences that would otherwise be uncharacteristic. My advice would be to allow your wife to express her thoughts and feelings without judgement. In time the memory will probably fade.'

'Probably? I'm not sure I like those odds,' said Stephen.

'It is entirely possible that the shock of this accident may result in some sort of religious awakening in your wife,' said the doctor quietly. 'A brush with death, a powerful hallucination, and a search for meaning, can send even the most intelligent people running into the arms of God. It wouldn't be the first time. Would that be so terrible?'

Stephen visibly squirmed.

'Give her time to think and time to integrate the meaning of this event into her life. Your wife is a journalist, when she has had a chance to examine this experience with some level of detachment I'm sure she'll come to the logical conclusion.'

Chapter 6

'What do you see?'

Wasn't Daniel supposed to be the one asking the questions? Clearly, this interview was going to be a learning experience. Peter Randall could hardly contain his excitement. He had held up the picture as soon as Daniel had taken his first sip of coffee.

The drive to New Jersey had left Daniel feeling stiff and tired. He should have stopped off at a diner before calling to the apartment. Now things had gotten off to a bad start. It was the mistake of an amateur to allow his subject to control the conversation. Daniel decided to throw the ball back into his court.

'Why don't you tell me what we're looking at?' said Daniel.

Peter Randall was happy to oblige.

'This is a print of a famous painting from the sixteenth century. It's called "Ascent into the Empyrean". Just take a look at the tunnel and the light at the end of that tunnel; see how the angels are guiding the deceased towards that light?

'This is a scene that's familiar to so many of us who have survived a near-death experience. But it wasn't painted by a recent NDE survivor, it was, in fact, painted by Hieronymous Bosch, a Dutch painter who was around long before anyone had ever heard of a near-death experience.'

Happy with that opening evidence, Randall continued his argument with another picture. Again, he held this print in front of his chest and presented it with all of the vigor of a parent who was hot-housing an infant's intelligence with flash cards.

'And look at this, this was drawn by the British painter and poet William Blake in 1808. The title probably tells you all you really need to know: "The Soul Hovering Above the Body Reluctantly Parting with Life". A classical out of body experience and a regular feature of most NDE experiences and we see it clearly depicted here in a nineteenth-century picture. How do the skeptics explain that?'

The 72-year-old was an evangelist with a mission.

Daniel tried to get the interview back on track. 'Those are very compelling images,' he said, 'but what I'm looking for is an account of your own personal experience. I'd like to start filming now if you're happy to talk about that?

Randall laid down the pictures and shifted forward in his chair, clearly eager to tell his story.

'What happened to me on February 14th 1980 changed my life forever. I was at the very peak of my career. My record as a litigator was impeccable. I was a very zealous advocate and my reputation for securing huge settlements for my clients meant that opposing counsel most often chose to settle cases before they even went to court. There was a lot of grandstanding involved. It was a game where the stakes were high. Those negotiations made me feel more like a Vegas high-roller than a lawyer in Manhattan. The buzz was intense.

'But I was a heart attack waiting to happen. I weighed 280 pounds, I smoked 40 cigarettes a day, and I'd developed quite a taste for brandy. The only vegetables I ever ate were sandwiched between hamburgers or in the toppings of late-night pizzas.

'Still, it never occurred to me to worry about my health. Maybe all of that power left me feeling immortal, I don't know.

'I was on my way to court when I stopped at a nearby diner for a quick lunch and a meeting with another lawyer. Jerry Connelly wasn't exactly my biggest fan. I'd cost his client some serious money the last time we'd met in court. This time he was keen to settle, though he tried to play it cool. We both knew he was going to pitch me an offer, but he refused to get straight to the point. I remember I was pissed to have to listen to him make a case he didn't have as I tried to enjoy a steak sandwich.

'The man had no charm, no charisma whatsoever; he just talked and talked. I noticed his Ivy league scarf and found a reason to like him even less.

'My heart attack didn't feel like a heart attack at first. You know you hear people say they felt like there was an elephant sitting on their chest? Well, it was nothing like that, not even close. At first I thought I was coming down with stomach flu or something. I felt nauseous and then there was this cold sweat. I thought I might puke or something, so I stood up to go to the john, and all this time Jerry's still talking. I swear, he didn't notice anything was wrong until I collapsed beside our table.

'His expensive education clearly had not equipped him to cope with an actual crisis. The guy just stood there completely clueless. It was a waitress who called 911. The pain had a grip of me by then. I remember looking up into Jerry Connelly's face feeling pretty pissed that the last sight I would ever see on this earth was that dumb schmuck.

'The pain was overwhelming. I shut my eyes and thought that I just couldn't take any more. And then, quick as a flash, I found myself looking down on the whole thing. I could see everything. I could read the name-tag of the waitress who started CPR. But I could see so much more than that. It was like I had 360 degree vision. I could see anything that happened to pop into my attention.

'Even walls were no obstacle to me. It's hard to explain. But I could simultaneously look at my body while I looked at the taxi driver who was yelling at a jay-walking pedestrian across the street. As I started to understand my new abilities I quickly lost interest in what was going on in that diner.

'I knew that the fat guy on the floor wasn't really me; and I knew that he never really had been. You know? My body was like a crumpled suit that I didn't need any more.

'Things were starting to make sense. I wasn't at all worried by what was going on. I didn't even care that I would probably never see the inside of a courtroom again. In fact, when I thought about it, I realized that my whole career in law had really been just a complicated game that the guy there on the floor had liked to play. It wasn't important. So, not going to court ever again was nothing to worry about.

'The thought crossed my mind that I had never made it to Rome. I'd always wanted to go to Rome, I'd always promised Pam I'd take her there one day, but you know how it is... When I was younger I didn't have the cash and then, when I had the cash there was never the time.

'And then the weirdest thing happened... I suddenly found myself in Rome. The Trevi Fountain was bubbling away right in front of me while I took in the view, like some kind of ghostly tourist. I knew I was really there. There was so much detail and life, I just knew I wasn't dreaming or imagining it.' Peter Randall laughed.

'My thoughts had allowed me to become manifest halfway across the world.

'Can you even begin to imagine what that felt like? It was a rush. I wished I could have shared the experience with my wife Pam. And then suddenly it was like, bam!

'Before I knew it I was looking down on Pam. She was at home in our apartment watching one of those crappy daytime soaps on TV, just like I always suspected she did. Funny, isn't it? I could have gone anywhere and instead I wind up back in my own apartment looking at the wife who I never really thought about.

'I wondered what would happen next, when I felt myself being lifted upwards. It's hard to describe, but suddenly I was in a tunnel. There was a light in the distance, but if I turned my attention round I could still see Pam. I had an impression of great speed, it was kinda like I was flying with no effort. The light got bigger and bigger. The closer I got to the light the happier I felt. Something inside of me knew I was going home. And I had the clearest sensation that I was not alone.

'I burst through the end of the tunnel and into the light. There was a feeling of euphoria and colors like I couldn't even begin to describe.

'Other people – just energies really – gathered round me. By now I had lost the illusion of a body and I moved as pure energy too. These other energies, or spirits I guess you could say, were able to communicate with me directly through their thoughts. They conveyed their love to me and they welcomed me home.

'I realized that I was returning from a mission and that it was time to bear witness to everything that I had learned.

'Time took on another dimension, because my entire life was played back to me in what felt like real time. But if it was the movie of my life then you would have to say that it was the director's cut with commentary, because not only were we seeing my life, but we were able to *feel* the consequences of my actions on those around me. It was hard to watch in parts. But the others did not judge me. I did not have to plead my case, instead I had to feel the pain that I had caused to those around me.

'It was the most vivid experience I have ever had. And when this review of my life ended I realized that I had forgotten the purpose of my life on Earth. I had become distracted by my narrow concept of the world. I had played life like a game that I intended to win. I felt like a real schmuck.

'Those other spirits completely empathized with my pain and distress. They told me that I could choose to have another chance. It wasn't too late for me to return to the world and to live the life that I had intended to live. And even though I understood that returning to the world would mean removing myself from that perfect environment, I knew immediately that's what I had to do. In the instant that I made my decision I felt myself being pulled back.'

Peter Randall paused and took a sip of water.

'It's hard to know how much of the pain I experienced on my return was caused by the loss of the love of those others in spirit and how much was the reality of returning to a body that had suffered a massive coronary.

'I woke up in the Emergency Room, surrounded by doctors who were surprised to see me open my eyes. According to the clock on the wall it was only 30 minutes or so since my collapse in that diner. But in those 30 minutes I had re-lived my whole lifetime; they'd changed my life.'

Daniel could see why Peter Randall had once been such a successful litigator; the passion of his storytelling bordered on the evangelical. But Daniel needed to ensure consistency in these interviews. He needed to control the flow of Peter's powerful relaying of his experience. It was the moment to ask another question.

'Were you a religious person before this experience?' he asked.

'I swore an oath on the Bible when I was called to the bar. The hospital's paperwork listed me as Presbyterian, but I always viewed religion as an accident of birth. My religious life was never an active choice but rather a sort of cultural inheritance. The Randall family just happened to be Presbyterian. That fact did not make the beliefs of their church seem any more true or relevant to me than any other.

'Though I never gave the subject much consideration, I'm sure I would have explained God away as an invention of ill-informed, superstitious minds. My world-view was more existential. I trusted only what I could see or explain and I never did delude myself with any expectations of an afterlife. So you can imagine how shocking this experience was for me...' he paused expectantly.

'How did the experience change you?' asked Daniel.

Peter Randall smiled broadly.

'It changed everything absolutely and irrevocably. There was no going back. It cut my life in two. There was the life of the litigator, who I hardly recognize now as myself, and then after my near-death experience, there was a sudden dawning of consciousness and an undeniable need to follow a more spiritual path.' He gave an emphatic look.

'Of course, Pam didn't understand. Not that I blamed her – if the tables had been turned I probably wouldn't have believed her either. Best thing she ever did was to divorce me a year after this happened, because it set me free to follow my own path.

'For a while I thought my purpose was to convince people that my story was the truth. I can only imagine that I came off sounded like some religious nut. And nobody listened anyway. So I gave up talking about it.

'I traveled for a while. You know, I did actually make it to Rome, not that it impressed me much…. I'd seen it all before, you could say! I guess I felt a little lost.

'My identity had always been so wrapped up in my job that I wasn't entirely sure who I was without my career. So I returned to New York to volunteer my services to a legal aid charity. But that didn't really work. The thrill of the game, or maybe the thrill that was the *illusion* of the game had gone. And that's when my Mom was diagnosed with pancreatic cancer.'

Daniel had never before seen anyone's face light up at the recollection of such tragic news. But Peter Randall was clearly happy to remember.

'Mom had refused to speak to me since the divorce,' he continued. 'She told me that I was flushing my life down the toilet when I left my law firm to go traveling. She said it was an expensive mid-life crisis and suggested I should get a grip and just get a mistress like any normal middle-aged man.'

Peter Randall laughed.

'So when I saw her looking so thin and so ill… my God she was a shadow of the woman she once was… She told me her nurse was a bitch – she still had some spunk left in her – and that's when I made the decision to nurse my Mom myself. It felt like the perfect solution to her problems and to mine. Right place, right time. So I moved in to her apartment – this apartment – and we spent those last few months of her life living all of the best days that we'd ever had the privilege to share.

'I muddled through all of the day-to-day chores that go with caring for someone full-time. In the last couple of weeks I even had to change her diapers... That's something that would have revolted me before my own experience.

'The man I was before would have paid any amount of money to a stranger to make sure that he didn't even have to think about such an ugly reality of life. But that feeling of revulsion just wasn't there. There wasn't a chore that didn't give me joy. I could sit beside the bedside of my dying mother and instead of noticing suffering, what I was feeling was pure love. There was no grief.

'Sharing my experience with her really helped her to make that final transition. It was beautiful to watch. There was no fear.

'In the moment when she finally passed I came to know my purpose. I knew why I'd been allowed to return to the world. And I knew that I could continue to serve others in that same way. That's how I came to re-train as a nurse in a hospice.

'It's light years away from the life I had before. I used to claim more on expenses in one week than I make now in an entire month...And I can't imagine a better life.'

Chapter 7

Ann was unsettled. Something was missing. Though she was relieved to be released from the hospital and grateful to be sleeping in her own bed in the Hamptons, without that clinical hospital smell, she did not feel as though she was truly at home.

There was no comfort to be found, not even in her own body. The pain was like a constant background noise that lulled her into limiting her movements and counting the minutes until it was time for her next painkiller. Things had seemed simpler when she had been in the care of the hospital. There the fundamental fight for her survival had seemed medicalized and beyond her control. Now, released from the constant comfort of the morphine drip, she was painfully conscious of the fact that nobody else could make the journey to a complete recovery for her. Despite the flurry of activity in her normally quiet sanctuary of a house, she knew she had to face this journey alone.

Her experience with pain had previously been limited to relatively minor and short-lived events that now seemed almost comical in retrospect. There had been a solitary, sleepless weekend when she had battled with the pain of a root canal.

Some years later, a horrible knee injury had resulted in a shortened ski holiday in Mont Tremblant and a knee that was (briefly) the size and colour of an eggplant.

Neither of these experiences had prepared her for the unrelenting and personality-distorting levels of pain that she was now experiencing.

She wondered how she had ever failed to have expressed some gratitude for the healthy and charmed life that she had once lived. There was no going back to that woman and to that life. She knew that. Her life had changed irrevocably. The physical injuries would mend in time, but what would happen then? Perhaps it was easier to concentrate on her physical pain than to contemplate the meaning of her brush with the Divine.

Besides, it was hard to be philosophical when she was only minutes away from her daily dose of tortuous physical therapy. Monica had challenged Ann's previous belief that physical therapists were sympathetic care-givers with a vocation to make people feel better. The woman was a scrub-faced sadist. Ann believed her wholesome look of leisurewear and neatly-bunched hair concealed a dark compulsion to contort the injured and the impaired into unnatural and excruciating ranges of movement.

Ann did not want to flex or rotate her hips. And she certainly did not need the daily visits of a cruel cheerleader to witness her suffering. She did not want to force her body into any position that would necessitate pain.

The irony of her situation was not lost on Ann. How many times had she interviewed survivors of disasters who had battled extreme odds and had remained remarkably positive? She had forged a career out of reporting on the suffering of others and yet, here she was, falling at the first hurdle. The first real test of her character was a catastrophic failure.

Every visitor that Ann had seen since the accident had used the same maddening and limited vocabulary. They told her that she was a fighter (who exactly was she fighting?) and that she must stay positive. Everyone told her that they just knew how brave she was (really?) and that she would be back to normal in no time.

The fact was, no one was listening to her.

Stephen had never been the sort of man to sit around holding her hand. He was a man of action. It was his old-fashioned masculinity that had attracted her to him in the first place. Their marriage had been a marriage of equals. Until now Ann had had quite enough people to listen to her every word. When millions of people were tuning in to hear your every deliberation it seemed unnecessary to partner with someone who would only add to your audience. Ann had never wanted a husband who would simply pander to her ego. They had come together fifteen years ago as two highly successful people. They each understood the demands of their respective careers. Success was the tie that bound them together.

Of course it was impossible to share so many years of intimacies without exposing some measure of vulnerability. Stephen knew Ann as she existed beyond the glamor of the studio. He had seen her through stomach flu, menstrual cramps and zits. When her name had not been called at award ceremonies, he had always been there to console her and motivate her. For her part, she had seen Stephen cry when his father had died. It was she who consoled him whenever he worried about his thinning hair.

But this was different.

This had the potential to be a deal-breaker.

If the tables were turned she doubted whether she would have thought any differently to Stephen, though she knew she would have made a better job of masking her doubt.

Her experience had taken her beyond the confines of her understanding of reality. Now she saw that her old faith in only that which she could see, touch, hear and feel in the material world had offered a steady comfort of sorts. When faith was limited to the visible and measurable parameters of the physical, it was easy to take comfort in the indisputable and the observable. A rational view of the Universe demanded evidence. There was no proof of a Higher Power. Nobody had ever even proved the existence of the soul. No wonder most religious believers sounded like fruitcakes.

Ann's experience of religion had been limited to the social aspect of church-going. Attendance at church most Sundays had given her Mom a platform to put her perfectly turned-out family on display. Even as a child, Ann had suspected that most people were there because they enjoyed the hymns. Church was a well-dressed singing club that offered the community an opportunity to gather and gossip. If God was present in any of the proceedings it was only ever as a lyric or a half-hearted recital of a prayer.

Years of attending church only when necessitated by weddings, baptisms and funerals had done little to alter Ann's cynical view of religious observance. The faith that she witnessed was polite and apologetic. Nobody had ever offered the opinion in her earshot that death was only an illusion. Her Christian upbringing had demanded nothing but charity and offered nothing but forgiveness for unspecified 'sins'. Talk of Heaven and life everlasting had been relayed as a comforting fable to the bereaved and the very young. The educated and the adult knew better.

No wonder nobody would listen to her now she had another view of reality. She claimed to have witnessed what many people professed to believe, but any talk of her experience would inevitably lead her to another appointment with a psychiatrist.

It hurt too much to think about.

She swallowed another painkiller and waited for Monica.

It was just too bad that the genie could not be returned to the lamp.

Chapter 8

Daniel did not celebrate Christmas.

There was no evidence of any seasonal festivities in his modest home. Years of military life had instilled a love of order and neatness in him that was clearly manifest in the clean, uncluttered surfaces. His only concession to the fact that it was Christmas Eve was the food that filled his refrigerator; pork tourtière and Quebec sugar pecan pie. The food hamper was a gift from an old friend of his Mom's. Amelie Rousseau was the closest thing he had to an aunt. Her mothering radar always somehow made her aware of his occasional visits to his old home. She had dropped by to invite him to that night's planned Réveillon. The Christmas food that she had brought was evidence of her doubt that she could ever persuade Daniel to join in the crowded celebrations.

Amelie Rousseau's visit had reminded Daniel of all that he had once loved about Christmas in Portland. The Christmases of his childhood had offered him a bright, warm respite from the severity of his mother's temper and the deprivation of the life that they shared in this shabby, old colonial house. Réveillon celebrations had shown his young eyes something of the girl who had somehow transformed into his embittered and joyless mother. He had watched his Mom join in the singing of the hymns of her native Quebec and although he understood little of the French that was banned in their household, he had felt a connection to her that otherwise eluded them both.

It had been years since his last Christmas in Maine. The failing health of Marie Breton had thrown mother and son together for one last Réveillon six years before. Despite the best efforts of Amelie Rousseau, Daniel had no happy memories of that last visit. The combination of his excessive drinking and his mother's acid tongue had allowed for no final reconciliation. Their parting had been as bewildered and angry as always.

Christmases in the Marines had offered Daniel something of the camaraderie that he remembered from those Portland Christmas celebrations of his childhood.

Not for the first time that day, Daniel wondered why he had returned to this empty, old house. Memories of his last Christmas with Fred and Joanna bubbled, unwelcome, to the surface.

It was the promise of solitude had lulled him back to this place, he supposed. He would not be fit to continue with his work unless he took some time alone to reflect.

Strange to think that it had only been two years since his world had turned upside down.

Daniel's return to Fallujah in 2006 had been unplanned. He thought that he had left the chaos and the devastation of that desert city behind the day he'd left the Marine Corps. But the divorce had been expensive. And civilian life was beyond his experience, so when a Private Military Contractor Company had offered him in excess of $1,000 per day to return to Iraq as a hired gun, he hadn't been able to come up with a reason to refuse their offer.

Mercenary was a dirty word. It conjured up images of dishonourable soldiers of fortune. Most Americans would have been shocked to learn that PMC operatives accounted for the second biggest armed force in Iraq at that time. They were a raggle-taggle group of men, 'private security' hired to protect oil experts, surveyors, building contractors and TV crews. Like Daniel, most of them had some experience of the sandbox. Some had, like him, once been grunts, there was a smattering of British ex-blades and a number of veteran soldiers.

But not every PMC operative had the necessary knowledge of urban combat to survive in such a hostile environment, let alone to protect an unarmed civilian. It was that disparity in experience that had troubled Daniel the most; knowing that he was operating beyond the discipline of the Marine Corps caused him to become ever more meticulous in the planning and execution of excursions through the streets of Fallujah.

Shepherding unarmed civilians was a responsibility that Daniel took very seriously.

The twisted logic of the US military had decided to invest $200 million dollars in reconstruction projects in Fallujah in order to convince the local population to side with coalition troops. Given that it was an attack of Marine-led US troops that had virtually destroyed the city only two years before, people were understandably suspicious. Death threats and executions were increasingly common against anyone seen to be doing business with the US military. No wonder that the civilians in Daniel's care had opted to travel through the city incognito. Travelling in a Marine-led convoy would have been the kiss of death to their hopes of meeting their reconstruction goals.

Daniel's experience in Fallujah had been invaluable.

Operation Phantom Fury had cost so many lives and had destroyed almost half of the unpainted cement houses and buildings in what was then a pit of vipers. But it had taught Daniel enough about the city to navigate unnoticed. As ever, it was the smallest details of planning that had the greatest impact.

Although he missed the protection of his Wiley X sunglasses with their ballistic lenses and toughened goggles, he had discarded his sunglasses (and he had instructed all in his care to do likewise) so that he would not be immediately marked out as a white eye and a westerner.

The same principle of sacrificing some measure of protection for the sake of anonymity applied to their choice of vehicles. They travelled in a convoy of low-profile vehicles, each a different color and make..

Daniel's preference was for old pickup trucks, sometimes he would even go so far as to further camouflage the truck with a cargo of livestock or vegetables. Although the bodywork of all their vehicles was beaten, the engines were always in excellent condition. Worry beads on the rear-view mirrors and stickers on the bumpers added to the authenticity.

Two heavily-armed PMCs travelled in each vehicle. Discretion was everything. Weapons were kept out of sight. Daniel kept his AK-47 on his lap at all times during these perilous journeys. He preferred it to the M16A4 rifle that had been issued by his employers. With so many lives on the line he had to have complete confidence that his weapon would handle the harsh desert conditions, and the AK-47 that he had salvaged from an arms cache was his weapon of choice. Access to the Soviet-built weapon was one of the few benefits of operating outside the control of the US Marine Corps.

Daniel was prepared to fight any threat of an ambush, but he knew that whatever preparations he might make, no road was ever really safe. There was the constant threat of an Improvised Explosive Device (IED). And he knew that he could not fight a bomb. All he could do was to recognize the risks. IEDs were usually hidden under piles of rubbish on the roadside. Some of the more inventive insurgents had been known to even hide them inside the carcasses of dead animals. But although trash clean-up contracts had been awarded to clear the roads of garbage and of easy places to hide bombs, most of the city's streets were still strewn with rubbish. The risk remained high.

It was on a December day in the week before Christmas that Daniel's worst fears were finally realized. He had chosen to abandon his favored position in the lead vehicle and, instead, had opted to ride with O'Leary in the second vehicle in the convoy that day. The ex-police officer and army reservist was the weakest link in the team. It wasn't O'Leary's lack of military experience that troubled Daniel (though that was a factor), his main concern was the emotion that he brought to the job.

Daniel had seen it all before. Like so many of the young bucks who had surged into the armed forces in the wake of 9/11,

O'Leary was on a mission for revenge.

He lacked the cool detachment that was essential in order to spot, or even survive an ambush. Daniel had known it from the first moment he had seen O'Leary pull the piece of World Trade Center rubble from his pocket (something he did before each trip).

It was the sight of a battered, black BMW (the kind generally favored by insurgents) in the wing mirror that had forced Daniel's attention from the road ahead. His attention had been distracted. And so he did not see the huge blast that tore through their lead vehicle. Instead he felt the enormous, scorched force of the IED as it impacted his truck with a violence that was both chaotic and deafening. Daniel had no time to respond to the shock of the explosion. His body was propelled through the windscreen of the pickup truck at a murderous speed.

His only thought, if he really did have time for a thought in that shocking moment, was to find his precious AK-47. These roadside bombs were almost always followed by an armed ambush. He had to be ready to protect the men in his care. Death was not an option.

But the illusion that Daniel had ever really been in control was probably the first casualty of the day. With no kevlar to protect him from the blast, he never had a chance of remaining conscious.

His crumpled body must have looked like just another bloody fatality to the war-weary citizens of Fallujah.

Chapter 9

Moira Richards sometimes felt like a time traveler. The world she occupied was so very alien to the world in which she was raised that the passage of a mere 72 years could not possibly account for the differences.

It bothered her that the young so often chose to judge her generation with a harshness that made no allowances for the way the world had worked before the rise of Oprah, blended families and the touchy-feely psycho-babble that lacked even the pretence of any core values.

It was different for Ann, she'd been born at just the right time, but she didn't know how lucky she was. She had been raised to entertain expectations beyond secretarial school and marriage. But pointing out her good fortune had always been a pointless exercise.

A combination of youth, beauty and intelligence had propelled her daughter forward into the world without so much as a backwards glance. Moira wasn't looking for gratitude exactly, but it worried her that Ann's phenomenal success had done nothing to keep her sense of entitlement in check.

Maybe the accident would be the first crack in the perfect life that Ann had somehow created almost effortlessly?

Moira was worried. Ann had survived the car wreck against all odds, but she now seemed to have lost her survival instinct. Something told Moira that her daughter would have to be taught how to fight for her life if she didn't want to lose everything.

Her own mother had always said that what doesn't kill you will make you stronger. And she certainly spoke those words from experience. Could any woman of Ann's generation truly imagine what it must have been like to have been widowed at the tender age of 22 with a baby daughter to support? Those women didn't waste time analyzing their feelings; they didn't fall to pieces when their husbands and lovers were slaughtered on the beaches of France – they knew that they had to simply put one foot in front of the other and just get on with the business of life.

Ann had inherited her sentimentality from her father. Peter had always had a tendency to indulge in his feelings. Father and daughter had had the sort of cosy relationship that excluded others.

It didn't surprise her that Peter had traded secrets with his daughter in order to boost their exclusive bond, but she had never expected him to sink so low as to have told Ann about Lauren. The idea of it almost made her want to vomit.

Hearing that name – a name that Peter Richards had insisted on giving their dead baby, despite the fact that the hospital assured them there would be no need for a birth or death certificate – pulled Moira back to a time that she had wanted to forget. She had been an innocent 23-year-old, full of nerves and excitement, waiting for the arrival of a baby that was ten days past its due date.

What would Ann have made of a maternity ward where smoking was permitted and mothers were encouraged to feed formula to their new babies? None of the young mothers on Moira's ward had consulted with their doctors about a 'birth plan'. They did as they were instructed by the medical personnel, and no woman would ever have thought to challenge the god-like status of the doctors. The doctors knew best and the women were grateful to be a new generation of mothers with the opportunity to deliver their babies in bright lit, clean hospitals.

Moira had planned for the birth with the dreamy zeal of a first-time mother. The glamor of her bed-jacket and her careful make-up had pointed towards her inexperience of all things maternal. Although she was somewhat worried about the pain, she did not allow herself to dwell too long on thoughts of the messier mechanics of childbirth. Her own mother had reassured her with a reminder that no matter how consuming the process of birth might be, it would all be over in a day and soon forgotten in the busy-ness of caring for an infant.

But it hadn't ended in a day; 32 hours of labor pains had left Moira an exhausted and ravenous shadow of the glamorous young woman who had felt the first contraction with a flutter of excitement. A succession of doctors and midwives had done little to hide their disappointment with her slow progress.

Of course, Peter was nowhere to be seen. In those days men were spared the horror of birth. So there had been no hand to hold hers when she had her first inkling of disaster.

The expression on the face of the midwife had told Moira everything she needed to know; her examination of Moira's huge, swollen abdomen with an ear trumpet had been conducted in a deathly silence. Things soon took on the speed and intensity of a rescue operation. Of course, nobody consulted Moira before the episiotomy. The medical team that quickly filled the delivery room displayed scant regard for anything beyond her uterus. She was simply told that they needed to get the baby out; and the huge, shiny forceps were produced as evidence of the obstetrician's intent.

It was funny how she had no real memory of the pain. The horror of the pain wasn't something that she had forgotten, exactly, but she could remember it only as fact rather than as a feeling.

She wasn't the sort of person to indulge in memories of personal tragedies, but on those rare occasions when she was forced to remember that day, she tended to remember the terrible silence that followed the delivery of her floppy, blue baby. She could still clearly remember the face of the midwife who had squeezed her shoulder in some display of consolation and assured her that she would have an angel in heaven.

What a stupid, ignorant woman. If Moira had had the strength she would have smacked her. How typical of the mindlessly religious to talk of angels and heaven when the sheer weight of tragedy was clear evidence that their ideas of a loving God were an absolute sham.

Peter hadn't seen her cry. He wasn't the one who had to deliver the afterbirth and who had to endure the stitches. Moira had been moved to a bed in a small side ward that was as far away from the crying of newborn babies as the staff could manage.

A nurse had handed her a hairbrush and cosmetics purse before Peter's arrival. Moira had somehow found the strength to bear the unbearable.

But Peter had ruined everything with his own selfish tears and talk of Lauren. It was easily the most unforgivable betrayal of their marriage. Why had Peter told Ann about Lauren?

And why had Ann conjured up a trip to heaven complete with doting father and sister?

It was strange how the dead were so often beatified by the living. Nobody ever spoke of the transgressions of those who had died. Perhaps if Ann had claimed a heavenly encounter with a father who had been honest about his duplicity and infidelities, Moira would have had cause to consider a spiritual awakening. But talk of her daughter's supposed brush with the eternal only confirmed what she already knew. Ann had never recovered from the death of her father. This was a spectacularly bad time to reawaken latent grief. Ann needed to focus on her own recovery.

Chapter 10

'They say some souls travel in packs. And that makes a lot of sense when you really think about it. I mean, we're all connected, so of course we're going to wind up hooking up with people who have similar lessons to learn. It's something we all agree to before we ever arrive on Earth.'

Daniel tried to hide his discomfort. It was exactly the kind of New Age talk that he hated. He had no wish to be associated with the sort of flaky individuals who indulged in magical thinking and superstitious rituals. Besides, unless he focussed his efforts on working with normal, believable people, these interviews would lack all credibility. For a moment he considered abandoning the filming.

'You think I'm full of shit, don't you?'

Gloria Cartwright was still smiling. Daniel was relieved to see that she was not offended by his hesitation.

'Maybe you could just share the story of your near-death experience. Let's avoid talking about your conclusions until you've told your story. How did it begin?'

Gloria's smile deserted her. She twisted her long brown hair as she stared off into the middle-distance searching for the memories.

'I met Richard when I was fresh out of college. It was my first job. I'd just moved to Boston and Beth, my house-mate, had gotten me an interview at the big law firm where she worked. I was hired on the spot. Man, Beth and I sure partied hard that night, I can tell you.

'It should have been the most carefree time in my life, and for a while it really was. Richard was an accountant and he joined the firm about three months after I did. He swept me off my feet. No man had ever paid me as much attention as he did, it was pretty overwhelming; He couldn't get enough of me. We dated just about every night. At work he would even call me from his office three floors above just to see what I was doing. Beth started to joke around and say he was my stalker...

'I was too flattered and too loved-up to see the warning signs. But when he wanted me to move into his apartment, it simply never occurred to me that I was putting myself in harm's way. We married in Vegas. It was a spur of the moment sort of thing. Richard said we didn't need friends and family, he just wanted me all to himself.

'Things changed as soon as he got that ring on my finger. It started out with comments about my clothes. First time he accused me of dressing like a whore, he said it with a smile. He somehow made his jealousy sound kind of protective. So instead of shirts, I wore sweaters and instead of skirts I wore pants. But nothing I did to please him was ever really enough...

'He would time my trips to the supermarket. If I were late there would be hell to pay. He'd accuse me of having an affair. It got to the point I couldn't even make eye contact with a waiter without provoking one of his rages. I learned to avoid going out. But I couldn't avoid the office's Christmas party. Nobody at that party could have guessed the totally degrading scrutiny I had to endure just getting dressed for that evening.

'We must have looked like such a happy couple. Richard danced with me all night – he wouldn't let me out of his sight. When my boss pulled me up to dance I knew there would be consequences. Things really escalated when we got home that night. Richard pinned me up against the wall and I thought that he was going to punch me. He was spitting with fury, calling me names that made me feel sick to my stomach. But he punched the wall instead of me – put his whole fist clean through it. And then the tears started. He sat slumped at my feet and cried like a little kid, and somehow I wound up consoling him. Crazy, huh?

'It was a combination of hope and denial that kept me there, I guess. Those tears of his gave me fresh hope. Even at that point I would have denied that Richard was abusing me. I wanted to think that he was just a loved-up, jealous guy with a temper. But once things got physical I knew I was only fooling myself.

'Beth guessed something was up. She followed me into the ladies room one afternoon at work and asked me to remove the scarf that was wrapped around my neck. She knew I was hiding something. When I showed her the bruises I felt so ashamed. But it was the look on Beth's face and the tears in her eyes that really broke my heart. It was the wake-up call I needed.

'Beth took control. She couldn't have been kinder. Even though I had withdrawn from her, my best friend had never abandoned me. She told me we'd get though things together.'

Gloria paused for a moment, but Daniel knew better than to interrupt.

'The plan was simple. My boss, Mr Pearce, was to take Beth and me down to the court house, claiming he needed some secretarial support.

'I didn't pack a thing – I was too scared to even think of smuggling my toothbrush into my purse, in case Richard noticed anything was up. It had to look to him like it was just a regular work day. But or course, there was no meeting at the courthouse. Mr Pearce had already arranged for a restraining order and Beth had booked tickets for a holiday in Miami. When Mr Pearce dropped us off at the airport he handed me an envelope with two thousand dollars in cash and told me to have a good time. He said he'd make sure that Richard understood that he could never come near me again, and he promised to pass him a letter I'd written explaining that we were over.

'Those two weeks in Miami were exactly what I needed. Beth must have blown her savings on the hotel. She took me shopping and for the first time in a long, long time I was able to buy what I wanted without worrying about the consequences at home. Mostly we just swam and sunbathed, but on the last night Beth took me dancing. It felt like old times.

'Going back to work was scary. But each day that Richard stayed away from my desk and didn't call was a huge relief to me. Beth had added extra locks on the door, so I felt pretty safe back in her spare room.

Again there was a pause. Daniel could see the emotional toll that the memory demanded of Gloria. There was a shift in her expression.

'He must have been watching the apartment because he seemed to just appear from nowhere, right behind us, one Saturday morning when we were struggling into the apartment with bags of groceries. Beth stayed cool. But as she went to dial 911, he closed the front door behind him and I knew we were trapped. He didn't even give Beth any kind of warning, he just walked right up to her while she was calling the police and he shot her straight through the heart.

'I knew he was going to kill me, but I was too shocked to even try to get away. There was blood pouring from Beth's mouth. All I wanted to do was to hold her hand. So I sat there in the blood and said goodbye to the best friend I'd ever known. I could see she was gone.

'Richard kept screaming abuse at me, but I was past caring or being scared. He was going to kill me but I wasn't about to give him the power to make me feel fear or shame any more. I wanted my last moments on Earth to be on my own terms.

'He shot me as soon as he heard the sirens.

'The really strange thing was that it felt as though I was snatched out of my body before the bullet even hit my chest. There was no pain, and with that came the relief and certainty that Beth hadn't felt any pain either.

'You'd imagine that it would be scary to find yourself in a dark tunnel after all that trauma, wouldn't you? But it wasn't like that at all. I felt like I was soaring. I wasn't alone. There was a beautiful presence beside me, helping to propel me towards the light. The closer I got to the light, the more giddy with excitement I became. Bursting through into the light was just total and complete bliss.'

A broad smile now replaced Gloria's troubled expression.

'Everything was light. There were colors and sounds of a beauty and intensity that I had never experienced on the earth. I was surrounded by these beings of light. They were all so welcoming and full of love for me. I had a feeling that I knew those beings... those souls. I could feel their love and reassurance.

'I knew they understood exactly what it was that I had just experienced, but oddly enough, I didn't feel too connected to what had just happened only seconds before in Beth's apartment. There wasn't a shred of shock or fear in me. I was just so elated to be in the light.

'As we all gathered together, we began to view the story of my life... There was no judgement of me or within me as we all watched the most intimate highs and lows of my time on Earth. It was clear to me that we were looking only for evidence of the lessons I had learned and the love that I had shared with everyone who I had ever encountered. There was no suggestion of shame or blame, even when my mistakes were laid bare for everyone to see.

'It was then that I remembered that I had chosen the life of Gloria. There were things that I could only learn by living all of those experiences. And yet, I could see that there was so much more that I could have learned and so much more love that I could have given.

'I had been connected to everyone in my life before I had even taken my first breath. We had all chosen to learn our lessons together – my parents, Beth, even Richard. Everyone in my life had been a teacher and a student, all on the same path, all of us together.

'It was then I asked if I could go back. I knew if I was allowed to go back that I could learn so much more. I wanted to extend my experience here.

'That thought alone seemed to propel me back. I remember being back in the tunnel for a moment, and then I remember nothing until I finally regained consciousness in hospital almost five days after the attack.'

'Did you tell anyone about what you had experienced?' asked Daniel.

'That would have been pretty hard to do while I was hooked up to a respirator,' Gloria smiled. 'Turns out the shot missed my heart, but it took more than half my right lung with it.

'Of course, the police wanted a statement from me as soon as I could talk. Mr Pearce made them wait until I'd recovered some strength, though. He told me Richard had shot himself before the police ever made it to the apartment. He told me that I was safe, but I already knew that.

'I didn't tell him or anybody else there about what I had experienced. It wasn't something that I would have believed if I'd been told it by someone who'd just been shot, so I didn't imagine that anyone would have any cause to believe me. And you know, I did not want to put my energy into persuading people that the trauma hadn't left me crazy.

'So I chose to bask in the glow of that special memory, that new truth that had been revealed to me, and to use the experience to heal me through all of that trauma and grief. It was a silent savior to me at that difficult time.'

Even Daniel could get that. 'How did the experience, and by that I mean the near-death experience, change you?' he asked her.

'It opened my eyes! Looking back I think I must have been sleepwalking through my life before this happened to me. But now I'm conscious. I see the world as a temporary school. You and me, we're students here. The trick, I think, is to be in the world but not of it. Everything is an opportunity for learning and for love. Not that I'm a saint, mind. I still have my faults, but at least I am aware of the mistakes I make and I try to do better. I try to find the beauty in everybody and also in myself.

'I'm holding down the same job I was doing five years ago, when all this happened. And for a time that bothered me. I couldn't see how I was making a difference. I felt a need to serve, if that doesn't sound too righteous. That's when I started volunteering at the shelter. Now I help women to rebuild their lives; the same way Beth helped me.'

'And how about church?' asked Daniel. 'Do you go to church?'

'I wasn't raised to belong to any particular church, though I was baptized. Since my experience I do sometimes drop in to the church around the corner from here. Sit there quietly. It gives me some comfort, though I'm hardly a regular there.'

Daniel turned off the camera to signal the end of the interview.

'Mind if I ask you a question?' asked Gloria.

'Why are you driving round the country conducting these interviews? What's your story?'

Chapter 11

Katherine Krukowski was a shameless operator. Ann would never have agreed to the visit, but her Mom had clearly been duped by the practised charm of the pushy producer. Stephen had not been sympathetic to Ann's protestations. He didn't understand Ann's need to maintain some privacy in their Hamptons home. The sanctuary of their beachside hideaway had already been invaded by any number of nurses, doctors and of course her Mom, since the accident – but Ann had her limits. Katherine Krukowski was not welcome.

Talk of Katherine's visit had opened the way for Stephen to reintroduce the topic of Ann's future work plans into the dinner conversation. It was almost ten weeks since the accident, and while Stephen's patience had not been in any obvious decline, he had been spending more and more time in their Manhattan apartment; too tired and too busy to tackle the Long Island Expressway.

Ann's health was no longer of any real concern. It was not unnatural or unkind, she supposed, that he should show some interest in her work plans.

But the fact was that Ann was in no hurry to return to the studio. Thoughts of work were strangely absent. There was absolutely no evidence whatsoever of the combination of ambition and ego it was that had previously fuelled her rise to the top. She simply could not imagine a future facing all of those cameras.

Stephen guessed that she had lost her nerve. He said it was natural for her to have some fears about getting out there again when she had been confined to the house for so long.

Being so far removed from the buzz of Manhattan and the adrenalin rush of work had dented her confidence. He'd seen it happen before, he said. A lawyer buddy of his had talked foolishly for a time of taking early retirement and traveling round the world when he had spent too long recuperating from transplant surgery. Of course, he'd returned to work in the end and had never had cause to regret that decision. It would be just the same for Ann.

So in the end Ann had agreed to Katherine's visit. She had wanted to make a gesture to Stephen that would offer him some reassurance, and she supposed, she was curious to know if her own disinterest in work was in any way based in fear.

Katherine's visit confirmed many of Ann's suspicions. On one level it was comforting to be reminded of the fact that the accident had in no way distorted her memory or judgement of Katherine's character. She was as utterly charmless and manipulative as Ann had remembered her. Within two minutes of taking a seat on the sofa in Stephen's study (the room was chosen as a compromise to Ann's diminishing boundaries), Katherine was talking about ratings. She spoke as if Ann had even the slightest interest in the sweeps. And as Ann listened to all the talk of broadcast competition, she became aware of the comic pointlessness of Katherine's obsession with what was, after all, just a news magazine show. Percentage changes in viewing figures were of no consequence to Ann. But somehow, Ann managed to maintain the appearance of an active listener.

Years of encouraging the powerful and the famous to share their thoughts while she provided a rapt audience of one were clearly working their magic on Katherine. But Ann was tuned out. She felt herself to be an observer to the scene. Her attention was drawn to the sound of the sea as it crashed violently onto the beach that lay just beyond the patio doors of the study. She had to concentrate to even maintain eye contact with Katherine when her attention was really elsewhere.

Now that her pain was receding, she often found such fascination in the everyday stuff of life The sense of curiosity that was at the heart of all journalists was now directed towards her immediate environment.

It was as if she was seeing the world with new eyes. She regularly spent hours gazing out to sea, grateful that the freezing February temperatures left the beach mostly empty of visitors. The scene from her window often took on the exquisite detail of a masterpiece, leaving the books that she attempted to study mostly unread. It was a revelation.

The frantic pace of Ann's existence before the accident had left no room for idle thoughts and awe inspired moments of wonder.

She had been so busy working on assignments and chasing goals that she had almost missed the entire point of her own existence. How seductive it was, and how interesting that the world applauded that brand of workaholism that left no real time for personal reflection. Talk of a spiritual life would, at one time, have sent Ann in search of a quick exit. Now she hungered for a contemporary who could share her awakening.

There had been opportunities before the accident – she saw that now. Reporters traded in exactly the kinds of catastrophes and scandals that caused even the most rational person to talk of God. She had previously viewed this as an act of powerlessness and desperation.

When errant politicians called on God's forgiveness she had always been untouched by such cynicism. Disasters that touched the lives of normal, hard-working people were another matter. An early mentor had advised her to always remember that she was a reporter and not a social worker. It was a sound principle that proved almost impossible to remember in the aftermath of tragedy and profound social injustice. There was a cost to maintaining a professional detachment and impartial veneer when presented with human suffering and loss. At some point she had simply forgotten to grieve the losses that she was called upon to witness at such close quarters.

Her reporting from Ground Zero had been award-winning. For a short time it had reminded her, and probably the rest of the country, of the unpredictability and fragility of life.

She had held Stephen closer each night, drank the best wine and told absent friends of her love for them. How else could anyone respond to days spent interviewing rescue workers as they searched through the rubble and nights spent at candle-lit vigils in the company of grieving wives and families? That particular brand of doorstep terror had sent many people looking for answers. People had quit their jobs, marriages had been ended and saved, spirituality had been discovered and a new breed of soldiers had been born.

The changes to Ann's life had been temporary. At some point the daily demands of life had transcended the horrific memories of that Tuesday morning. Those like her, who had survived the tsunami of dust and debris that had threatened to engulf lower Manhattan, who had thought that they might never emerge from the nightmarish darkness that had so nearly swallowed them all, had somehow betrayed the lessons they learned that day. The fragility and unpredictability of life had been forgotten. Gratitude for the routine and the mundane stuff of life had quickly evolved into familiar feelings of entitlement and expectation.

Her memories of that time had an almost religious quality. It had been a disaster of almost biblical proportions. She had walked the surrounding streets in what looked to be the aftermath of a hellish tickertape parade, conscious that she was at once reporting on and participating in the most shocking news story that she had ever known.

In the days that followed, many of the most desperate bereaved people had sought some comfort in faith. She had witnessed the tireless work of the chaplains who had blessed the remains of those recovered from the smoking pile of rubble that had been at the very broken heart of New York City.

It had been Ann's privilege to meet many of those chaplains as they had counselled rescue workers who sought rest and refuge in St Paul's Chapel. She had wondered at their capacity to bring comfort and hope in the face of such mammoth loss. It was the only point in her life when she had wished for such a faith.

One particular memory stood out in her mind. A potent mix of grief and exhaustion had somehow broken through Ann's professional emotional armour one evening.

It was less than a week after the attack on the twin towers and Ann had taken a break in the chapel. Music – was it Mozart? – had flowed around the old church. Someone was playing the grand piano while firemen rested on cots that lined the perimeter of the church.

Ann had felt a sudden rush of gratitude for everyone in the chapel. There were doctors tending to the tired and the injured, chaplains prayed with some people while other volunteers provided food and drink. They were all connected in a common purpose.

There was goodness in the face of such terror. The beauty of the music confirmed the sacredness of the space and of the moment.

As she had sat there Ann became conscious that she was in the presence of God. It was an idea that was so beyond her understanding and belief that Ann had later dismissed it as a symptom of her own exhaustion and a sign of her sentimentality which she usually managed to keep hidden – even from herself. She had allowed herself only the briefest of brushes with the divine before she had returned to work, careful to remind herself that the terrorists who had been responsible for all of the carnage that she had witnessed had believed that they were acting on God's will.

Katherine Krukowski was still talking. It sounded as though she was making big plans. Did she take Ann's silence as acquiescence? What was she talking about? There was definitely some talk of Katie Couric's decision to share her colonoscopy with viewers. Wouldn't Ann like to share the story of her rehabilitation with their viewers? Maybe for the May sweeps?

No. No she wouldn't like to share the story. She was firm on that. Ann still knew how to say No to her shamelessly pushy producer. That was a relief.

Chapter 12

Daniel didn't even know how Mrs Gallaher got his cell phone number. It didn't matter. As soon as he heard that Fred needed him, he got in his car and headed south. He drove, stopping only for gas, until he reached the town of Northport, Long Island. It was six o'clock in the morning when he finally pulled up outside the house. He was surprised at how easily he had remembered the address. It had been seven years since his last visit. He had been surprisingly nervous then too. He'd never before been a Best Man. The social niceties of the role had left him feeling unnerved. This time he didn't know what to expect.

He switched off the engine and sat for a while wondering if it was too early to knock. Mrs Gallaher appeared at the front door, already dressed. Something told him that she hadn't had any sleep either.

Mornings were never kind to any but the very youngest of faces. Fred's Mom looked a good 20 years older than she had looked on her son's wedding day.

As she quietly ushered Daniel inside he noticed that her smile didn't reach her eyes. The smell of coffee filled the house. Daniel followed the trail of the aroma that led into the kitchen.

People often stared at the scar that now ran from the left side of his forehead to his jaw, but most people made some attempt to conceal the intrusion of their curiosity. Mrs Gallaher did nothing of the kind. Her gaze ran along the length of his scar in open grief. She reached out her hand to caress his jaw in maternal consolation.

'Poor baby,' she said. 'You're still a handsome boy. Sit down, I'll pour you some coffee.'

'So where is he now?' asked Daniel.

'Sleeping,' said Norah Gallaher as she sat and faced Daniel across the cluttered dining table. The too-bright light from the overhead lampshade did nothing to hide her weariness. She held on to her coffee mug as though for support.

'What exactly happened?' asked Daniel.

'I can't say I know the full story,' she said. 'Only what I can piece together from Freddie and the calls I made to Joanna. First sign I had of trouble was when he showed up here two days ago. I almost didn't recognize him... For a moment there I actually thought a homeless person had broken into my basement. I got home from work and saw one of the windows down there had been forced. I locked myself in my car and started to dial the police when I saw him walking towards me. He must have been living and sleeping in those same clothes for the past three weeks.'

'Why?' asked Daniel. 'Did he have some sort of bust-up with Joanna?'

'Sounds like they've been having problems for a while, but this is so much worse than that. Now he's in trouble with the law too. And he's just so broken Daniel, that I don't know how I can ever piece him back together.'

'Mrs Gallaher,' said Daniel as he extended his hands towards hers.

'Dear God,' said Norah Gallaher, regaining some of her composure, 'if I'm going to sit here spilling my guts out to you, then the least you can do is to call me by my God-given name – it's Norah. Okay?'

She smiled through her tears and took a deep breath.

'I thought the move to Florida would be good for both of them. Joanna's Dad has a business down there and he gave Freddie a good job with all sorts of prospects. As a mother, I was just so thrilled to know that Freddie got to spend his days in an office where nobody was going to shoot at him or bomb him again.

'We all knew he'd miss the Marines. But that last injury he picked up in Iraq put an end to all that – and I can't say I was sorry. A limp seemed like a small price to pay to get my son out of harm's way.

'Florida was supposed to be the making of him... So how did it come to this? I know my son is no saint, but I've never known him to have a drink problem. Have you Daniel?'

Daniel shook his head and said nothing, he wanted Norah Gallaher to continue. He needed to know what exactly had happened to his best friend.

'Joanna said he'd been using drugs too. She said he was just lucky that he was just drunk and not high when the cops pulled his car over. He swerved through three lanes of traffic on the highway – it's a miracle no-one was hurt. He was three times over the legal limit when they tested him and that was at eleven o'clock – can you imagine that? They kept him locked up until his arraignment.

'Joanna's Dad posted bail. They went down to the courthouse to take him home, but he just took off. He told Joanna that the marriage was over. She said he even tried to punch her Daddy. They thought he'd just disappeared off with some of his drinking buddies, she said he'd been doing that a lot lately.

'Somehow he made his way from Miami to Long Island. He says he hitched rides. And when he got here he looked like he'd been sleeping rough. He hadn't washed for weeks.

'It wasn't until I'd gotten him cleaned up and sober that I saw just how far gone he was. I called the VA hospital when I realized he needed to see a doctor, but they couldn't give me an appointment with a psychiatrist for another month and I'm not sure he can wait that long.

'I just don't know what to do Daniel. You know him better than anyone else. Maybe he'll talk to you. I don't know. Can you stay for a while and help me figure out what kind of help he needs?'

The tears came quick and fast then. Norah Gallaher made no attempt to hold back her grief and shock. For the first time since her son's return, she allowed herself to really feel.

Daniel was glad she had called. He would do whatever he had to do to save Fred.

Chapter 13

Ann's career in journalism had taught her that successful reporters were less concerned with the truth than they were with the story. But somehow, her years of experience counted for nothing when she was faced with the personal challenge of convincing Stephen of the reality of her experience.

The pre-accident Ann would have known that it was a mistake to even try to prove matters of faith and belief. Her husband did not believe her – was that so bad? It was not as though he thought she was a liar. His scepticism was based on his experience of the world and on the theory that her injured brain had somehow conjured up a comforting and eerily realistic dream.

Even if she had managed to convince him, did she really imagine that he would join her on some new spiritual adventure? Perhaps if Ann had taken the time to consider her motivation for gathering the evidence that she believed would justify her claims, she might have better understood her distress at the rift that had been created in her marriage. If the bond of a marriage was based on faith and trust, did that mean that Stephen must accept the truth of her experience? Or did Ann simply recognize that the life-changing nature of her revelation had far-reaching consequences and she wanted to ensure that she and Stephen would continue to travel in the same direction? Could life ever offer such guarantees?

Her investigation had been conducted through lawyers. She knew better than to trust any of the researchers that Katherine had put at her disposal. Besides, a near-fatal pile-up involving a celebrity of her stature had resulted in an inevitably huge amount of litigation. The lawyers had easy access to all the participants in the accident. Their questions would not arouse any suspicions.

She was almost giddy on the evening when she planned to present Stephen with her findings. Her Mom had gone to visit some friends in Connecticut for the weekend. Apart from Anita, who was preparing their meal, they would have the house to themselves. The weekend would mark a new beginning.

She arranged the papers in Stephen's study. It was important to deliver her findings with an authority that would leave no doubt as to her gravity or mental health. A giddy demeanour would only distract Stephen from the irrefutable facts of her case.

She was dressed for business. She had swapped the comfort of her leisurewear for tailored black pants and a white silk shirt. Her face was freshly made-up. Strange, how little effort it took to transform her appearance into the woman she had once been.

There had been no surprise for her when she had first read the accounts of the accident, but there had been a relief. She had never doubted the truth of her experience, but Stephen was a man who dealt with facts and figures. The laws that governed Stephen's universe were logical, provable and elegantly mathematical. He had studied structural engineering, not business, at university. And he still took pleasure in explaining to Ann the physics that accounted for the improbable but undeniable stability of bridges, domes and sky-scraping buildings that appeared to contradict the laws of gravity.

His huge intelligence, his questioning mind and his trust in all that was provable would help Ann to make her case. It was hardly surprising that he had been so dismissive of her babbling in the hospital.

This would be different. She would appeal to his sense of logic.

The evening started well. When Stephen saw Ann he mistakenly thought that the promise of a seduction was in the air. He pulled Ann to him and ran his fingers through her hair as he kissed her gently on the lips.

'Looks like somebody is getting back to business,' he said. 'You'll be back in Manhattan in no time.'

Ann smiled and carefully sat on the couch.

'I have news,' she said. 'Sit down here next to me. There's a scotch on the table.'

Stephen loosened his tie, undid his top collar button and sat next to Ann.

'Should I be worried?' he joked. 'The offer of a seat and a strong drink doesn't usually bode well.'

Ann squeezed his hand and flashed him a reassuring smile before picking up the first of the documents that lay before her on the coffee table.

'I've been doing some investigating...' she began.

'I knew you'd feel better once you started thinking about work again,' Stephen said.

'No sweetie,' she said, 'this has nothing to do with work. This is about the accident. I don't know why it took me so long to finally do some fact-finding for myself. I mean, I've spent my adult life investigating other people's dramas, right?'

'I don't know where you're going with this,' said Stephen. 'We know everything there is to know about what caused the accident. What's to investigate?'

'I'm not talking about what caused the accident. I'm talking about what happened to me after the accident.'

Stephen's expression changed.

'Ann, I thought we agreed to let that go.'

'Let that go! Let that go? Stephen do you even realize what you're saying? How could I even begin to let that go?'

She took a breath. It was important to keep her cool. This was a case to be proven, not some mission for conversion.

'I have proof,' she said, looking Stephen straight in the eye. 'These statements that I have obtained through our lawyers substantiate everything that I have said.'

'What?' said Stephen. 'now I'm supposed to believe that God's in the business of issuing affidavits?'

'You know that's not what I mean,' Ann snapped.

This was going to be tougher than she had thought. She had to hit him with the facts before he stopped listening.

'Remember in the hospital when I told you about the red pick-up truck? Well, I have a photo from the scene. There was a red pick-up truck flipped on its side. Just look right here,' she said, producing the photograph.

'It was driven by a woman, just like I said. Her description fits. And her dog was killed that day. It was a little Yorkshire Terrier and his name was Archie. Read the facts for yourself. Do you really think that I dreamed all of this up?'

Stephen didn't look excited. He just looked sad.

'So obviously you didn't dream up this part of your story,' he said. 'You must have spotted the woman and her dog in the pick-up truck before the accident even happened.'

'The pick-up truck was behind us,' Ann protested.

'So you overtook it! You saw the driver. You saw the dog. Okay, fine, the conscious part of your brain doesn't remember any of that now, but in the shock of the accident you remembered.'

'I knew the dog's name. I knew that he died,' said Ann.

'Maybe, when you were unconscious, you heard her calling for her dog,' Stephen said.

'The limo was over 50 feet away,' said Ann. 'Why can't you accept the fact that I saw this woman after the accident when I was out of my body?'

'Can you even hear yourself?' said Stephen exasperated. 'This experience has clearly interfered with your capacity for rational thought. Why would you even begin to settle for an explanation that defies logic? You're so much smarter than that.'

Ann stared for a moment at her husband, then, holding back the tears, she placed another photograph on the table.

'This is the rescue worker I described to you,' she said. 'Read his account of the accident, it is exactly as I told you. Exactly.'

Stephen wrapped his arm around Ann, as if to console her.

'Let's not do this now,' he said. 'The most important thing right now is for you to put all of your energy into making a full recovery.'

'I saw Lauren,' said Ann defiantly as she shook herself free from Stephen's consoling embrace.

Stephen stood up and poured himself another scotch.

'I think your Mom has already covered this territory with you,' he said. 'Frankly I think it's unfair of you to keep throwing this in her face when it causes her such pain. People didn't talk about things like stillbirths back then – but they did whisper. I don't know whether you heard about your dead sister from a gossiping relative or your Dad. But I do find that explanation a lot more plausible than the possibility that you were first introduced to your sister on some day trip to Heaven. And if you were really thinking rationally, so would you. Ann. Why can't you just let this go?'

'Why can't you just believe me?' asked Ann.

'Because you might just as well ask me to believe in Santa Claus or the Tooth Fairy.' Stephen's voice was raised now.

It was their first fight since the accident. Stephen felt flushed with shame for shouting at Ann when he remembered the desperation he had felt at her hospital bedside only a few weeks before. This was not what he had planned for their first weekend alone together.

'I love you,' he said. 'And that's all that really matters. We've both been under a lot of strain since the accident. Fighting isn't going to help anything right now.'

Ann kissed her husband.

It was in that moment she decided that some journeys are best made alone.

Chapter 14

Saving Fred had been his mission, but in the end he had failed. Those last ten days in Northport became one long, last goodbye. Fred became another invisible casualty of war.

There was no field manual, no standing orders on how best to bring a man back from the brink of insanity, so Daniel had been forced to rely on his own keen survival instinct and on his intimate knowledge of his friend.

Had he known that he was fighting a losing battle all along?

He had the strength and the experience to protect Fred in any battlefield, but in the end he had been unable to protect his friend from his own demons.

Daniel was in unfamiliar territory. He had known as much from the moment he set eyes on his sleeping friend, back home in his old room. How strange that he had never before seen his best buddie with civilian hair and a full beard. The bloated, blond-haired figure sleeping in the twin bed that faced his looked only vaguely familiar.

They all knew about Post Traumatic Stress Disorder. The modern face of the Marine Corps paid lip service to the idea of mental health. But in the end, offers of counselling and support were only mentioned in all too brief de-briefing sessions when thoughts of homecomings were paramount in everyone's minds. Invitations to report feelings of trauma and depression with a superior officer were treated with distrust. After all, who would want to arm a nut job?

The fact was that 21st century sensibilities could not sanitize any field of war. There was no cure, no eraser, no magic pill that would make difficult memories disappear.

It was impossible to witness and participate in the bloody reality of battle without experiencing a fundamental change in your identity. All warriors understood that simple truth. Each had their own way of coping with the more difficult memories. Some were healthier than others. There were things that Daniel had seen and things that he had done that he wished he could forget. But those things did not consume him. Fred, no less strong and no less able than his friend had clearly cracked under the strain. He had crossed a line.

At first the joy of their reconciliation had masked the full extent of the problem. The two buddies had a lot of catching up to do. Daniel knew better than to overwhelm Fred with questions. In any event, he didn't have to wait too long.

It was on the second night that the hallucinations began. At 3am he woke to find Fred shouting and kicking his bedding to the deck, convinced that there was a camel spider in the room. Just for a sleep-filled second Daniel almost panicked to think that the murderous desert spider (more scorpion than spider really) had invaded their quarters. But of course, they had left the camel spiders many thousands of miles away when they had left Iraq. Daniel quickly came to his senses and turned on the light. But that did nothing to ease Fred's hysteria.

Daniel reassured Norah as best he could when she was woken by the screaming. He sent her back to her room while he set about stripping the room of hiding spaces for spiders. It was a rational approach to a crazy terror, but it helped to calm Fred a little. As soon as the screaming eventually subsided, Fred curled himself into a foetal position and cried.

Contrary to public perception, the macho world of the Marine Corps was not hostile to male tears. In the close-knit brotherhood of the Corps men frequently had reason to cry – the birth of a baby, the loss of a loved one or the sheer frustration of operating in a hostile environment. But Fred's tears were different. Fred cried in fear, and it was the raw, uncensored display of his complete terror rather than his tears that was so very alien to Daniel.

'It was just a dream,' Daniel said as he pulled a quilt over his friend.

'Bullshit,' said Fred.

'Trust me,' said Daniel, 'there are no camel spiders in Long Island. We left them in the sandbox. They're half a world away from here.'

'Maybe they're a lot closer than you think,' said Fred, wiping his eyes. Though fully conscious he was still clearly haunted by his nightmare. He sat up suddenly and threw the quilt on to the floor.

'Man, I need a drink,' he said.

Daniel did not object. He followed his friend into the kitchen and took his place at the table. Fred stood by the open fridge and guzzled half a bottle of beer before passing another to Daniel.

'Sometimes I wonder, you know?' said Fred. 'Why did I survive? Why me? There were so many times when we were clearing houses in Fallujah when one different turn would have left me taking a bullet in the head instead of some kid you know? It was all so totally random...which corner to turn, which door to enter... The muj just sat and waited. They were so quiet we never knew where. They could have been behind any door... any door. I opened as many doors as anyone else. So how come I'm still here when so many others went home in body bags? Why did I survive?'

Daniel swallowed the cold beer.

'You just got lucky, I guess,' he said. 'Well, at least until that RPG hit your Humvee.'

'It was so fucked up,' Fred said. 'They didn't engage us like real soldiers. They didn't care if they lived or died just so long as they took an American with them.

'It was like no-one had ever explained the basic rules of warfare to them. How do you engage an enemy who wears no uniform, who hides behind women and children and who is so hopped up on adrenalin and amphetamines that they refuse to be killed?'

Daniel shrugged and allowed his friend to continue talking.

'What really got me,' said Fred, 'was how they would always go for the face. They knew better than to shoot at the vests, so they went for the face instead... There was one kid in my unit who got trapped in a house we were clearing. We had to practically bulldoze the place just to get him out. His best buddy couldn't even recognize him after they'd shot him up. He was nineteen – fresh out of SOI. I cleaned his kevlar and his weapon myself. I didn't want his friends to have to deal with all that blood...

'I thought about Private O'Dowd again when they medevaced me. I was on a stretcher in the back of a C-17. There was another kid there, surrounded by medics most of the way to Germany; half his head was gone. Just blown away. I don't know how they were keeping him alive. And for the five hours of the flight he just cried and cried for his Mom, just like a little preschooler. He cried for his Mom with half his brain missing. He would have been better off dead.'

Fred gazed into nothingness as he finished off his second beer. Daniel saw his opportunity to ask the question that had hung between them since his arrival.

'The drinking and the drugs,' he said, 'do you do them to forget about the things you saw?'

Fred turned his gaze to Daniel.

'It followed me home,' he said. 'I couldn't explain it to Joanna. We'd be in a crowded shopping mall and suddenly I'd be pumped up, sweating, looking for a suicide bomber. So, you know, I started to avoid crowds. Then I'd be on the highway looking out for IEDs. Crazy, huh? That day, when the cops pulled me over? I was swerving to avoid a cardboard box. But how can I explain that to some cop in Florida? I know it sounds crazy. My head is so screwed up.

'This,' he said, holding the bottle of beer, 'is just medicine.'

'I don't think the medicine is working,' said Daniel.

74

'It's all I got,' said Fred.

'There's a VA program to treat PTSD,' said Daniel. 'I've spoken to someone there, someone I know, and they have a place for you there next week... if you want it. It's a residential program. They can help you if you just give them that chance. Can I tell them you'll be there?'

Fred stared out of the kitchen window.

'I guess it beats a bullet in the head,' he said. But Fred did not sound convinced.

Daniel knew that he would have to remain vigilant until Fred was safely in the care of the Veterans' Association.

There were no weapons in Norah's home. Still, Norah removed any surplus medication while Daniel locked away all gardening tools and ropes.

Each day brought them closer to the promised safety of the treatment program. Nightmares and hallucinations decreased in both frequency and severity. Seeing these improvements, they made the fatal mistake of letting down their guard.

A drop in vigilance just two days before Fred was due to enter the program was all it took to allow him to steal the keys to Norah's car.

Hearing Norah's screams, Daniel rushed straight from the shower. In the moments it took him to race to his car, Fred had vanished. Daniel drove around the neighbourhood feeling increasingly desperate. Somehow he knew. He knew before they saw the police patrol car pull into Norah's driveway.

Fred had been seeking a release from his pain when he had raced Norah's car down the expressway. The illusion that death would bring an end to his life had led him to point his old toy gun at the patrolman.

Although, in the end, the bullet that had penetrated Fred's heart was fired by the police, it was, unarguably, a case of suicide.

Daniel had failed Fred. He had failed to share with him the

lesson that he had learned in Fallujah – that life never ends. No bullet, no rope and no knife could ever destroy a soul.

There was no 'over'. There never could be.

Chapter 15

Ann's decision to return to Manhattan was rooted in conflict and anger. The argument with Moira had been the final straw. Just the fact that she had actually chosen to confide in her Mom should have set off alarm bells. Experience had taught her that confiding in her Mom was like offering a bare neck to a wolf. It always ended badly.

She had gone looking for sympathy. The argument with Stephen had taken its toll on Ann's emotional reserves (and clearly, her judgement).

Although Ann had never known depression, she had suddenly felt faced with a void from which there was no escape. If she had been thinking straight she would have called a friend or even a therapist. But her Mom had been there – in the right place at the wrong time. And Moira Richards had a long-established talent for smelling weakness. It was uncharacteristic of her Mom to offer to walk with Ann along the beach. She normally avoided any unnecessary exposure to weather conditions that would play havoc with her hair. Cold empty beaches were an anathema to her.

A more rational and emotionally resilient Ann would have seen the signs and wondered at her Mom's agenda. But she had instead talked on and on like a starlet without a publicist. She had responded to her Mom's concerned clucking with an unguarded confession of her marital problems and her uncertainty about returning to work.

At no point did she ask her for advice. Anyone with the slightest degree of emotional intelligence would have understood that she was simply looking for empathy and not an instruction manual on how to live her life. But Moira Richards had obviously been waiting for an opportunity to offer her daughter some guidance and she was ready to pounce. The assault began with a familiar character assassination of Ann's Dad.

'Men are weak,' said Moira as she gathered the fur collar of her coat closer around her elegant neck. 'And I don't just mean that they're more easily seduced – which, of course they are. But they never really grow up, you know. They're all just potentially badly behaved boys, no matter how smart or powerful they are. Every man needs a woman to keep him in line. And Stephen is no exception. If your Dad had been left to his own devices, he would have been so busy chasing skirts that he would have had no time for his law practice and he never would have known the true pleasure of family life. He needed me, just like Stephen needs you.

'Women are made of tougher stuff. And that's not to say that it's always easy to keep a marriage together. Don't imagine for one minute that I didn't hurt all those times when your Dad behaved badly. Sure, I had my feelings. But you know, I never forgot the bigger picture.

'There are some times in life when we simply do not have the luxury of indulging in our feelings. There are some times in life when we must be stronger than we would like. I've been there and I know how hard it is. But sweetheart I really do believe that this is one of those times in life when you have to put your feelings aside and do what's right for your marriage and your career.'

Ann stopped in her tracks and faced her Mom. She realized she had been taken hostage.

'You think Stephen is cheating on me?' she asked.

'No, no, not at all,' said Moira. 'Though my experience has led me to believe that most men are incapable of monogamy. I'm not saying that Stephen is *cheating*. But I do believe that you are in danger of putting your marriage to a wonderful man at risk if you do not pull yourself together.'

Ann was surprised to find that she was capable of feeling

worse than she had felt before leaving the house.

'You lead a very charmed life,' said Moira. 'Never forget that there is a long line of women who are as beautiful and smart as you are who would sell their very souls to have your marriage, your job and your homes. I don't want to see you lose everything just because of the accident. You need to fight for what's yours. Defend your life before it's taken away from you.'

It was hours later, lying in bed, before Ann was able to compose some sharp and witty ripostes to her Mom's argument. But it was too late by then. The moment had passed and her Mom was on a flight back home to Arizona after quickly pronouncing her daughter fully recovered and no longer in need of mothering.

The anger that grew within her was a strange relief from her depression. How typical of Moira Richards to find a poisonous cure to her daughter's suffering. Unable to vent her rage and frustration, Ann became agitated and restless. She was no longer able to find peace in her surroundings. Her attention continued to return to her frustrations with her Mom. All thoughts of her spiritual awakening vanished as she focused her attention on the twisted mother / daughter relationship that had bewildered both Ann and Moira Richards for many years.

When Stephen called to say that he would be spending the night in their Manhattan apartment, she found a new focus for her fury. She told him nothing of the argument with her Mom. Any barbed comments that she might have made were swallowed back in the realization that she had become far too reliant on Stephen to meet her every need. It was time for action.

The irony that her decision to return to Manhattan would look as though she was heeding her Mom's advice was not lost on Ann. But the fact was she was returning to the city to regain some sense of independence and some fresh sense of herself. Stephen was not her nursemaid, and she would not become a recluse in her home in the Hamptons. Her salvation would only be found by taking some sort of action.

Anita was surprised to hear news of Ann's decision the next morning. Once Ann had told her, and the business of packing had begun, she became aware that it was too late to change her mind. She wondered how she would feel on the ride into Manhattan. The journey would take her past the accident site. It wasn't something that she wanted to face alone. She asked Anita if she would make the journey with her before she even had time to worry that she might appear needy. Things were changing. Ann still had the power to make things happen. And if she managed not to think too hard about everything, she was sure she would be strong once more.

The rain slowed traffic on the Long Island Expressway to a crawl. Ann was grateful to be travelling at a careful speed. She had not expected to feel so claustrophobic in the back of the limo. Her car trips since the accident had been limited to doctors appointments and hospital visits. Those relatively short journeys had been made when the distraction of her physical pain and medication had masked any anxiety that she may have felt about being a car passenger once more.

They were approaching the spot of the accident. Ann's heart felt as though it might explode. She wondered why she had ever imagined that she was ready to return to the city. Maybe she would never be ready. Was it possible that she would ever again be able to view the commute as an inconvenience and an opportunity to get some work done? Shouldn't her newfound enlightenment have made her immune to such feelings of panic and juvenile arguments with her Mom?

If she had had the courage, she would have grabbed Anita's hand for some comfort. But she could not imagine the consequences of such an intimate gesture with a woman who was, after all, her employee. Instead, she found distraction, as she so often had before, by launching into interview mode.

'Is your Mom alive?' Ann asked.

Anita shook her head. 'She died eleven years ago. Liver failure.'

'I'm sorry to hear that,' said Ann.

'Don't be,' said Anita, 'she was a wicked old bat. Drank herself into oblivion and blamed everyone but herself. I haven't been back to England since the funeral.'

'Mothers and daughters,' said Ann, 'it's not always easy, is it? Is that why you never had a family?'

Anita paused for a moment.

'Forgive me,' said Ann. 'I pry when I'm nervous, it's a bad habit.'

'I did have a family actually,' said Anita. 'If she had lived, my daughter would be 22 now. I often wonder what she would have looked like. They have computer programs that can simulate how people will age. I do that in my head sometimes. I wonder what kind of job she would have wanted to do. But she died when she was seven. She had leukaemia.'

Such a monumental and unexpected disclosure in a studio interview would have been down to seriously sloppy research work. Anita had worked for Ann for over five years. How was it that Ann had been so busy investigating the lives of whoever was deemed 'newsworthy' that she had neglected to discover such a hugely important fact about a woman who shared her home? Ann's feelings of panic were quickly replaced by shame and embarrassment. The hand she offered to Anita was one of consolation.

'I am so sorry. I had no idea.'

'You weren't to know,' said Anita. 'It's not something I usually talk about. I moved to America a year after Emily died. I thought that putting an ocean between me and my grief would help. But I still miss her every day. I still imagine what might have been.'

Anita gave Ann a reassuring smile. 'At least I know she's in a better place.'

'You believe in life after death?' asked Ann.

Anita nodded. 'It was the strangest thing. Those last few days with Emily actually gave me strength. I'd never seen anyone die before. The doctors didn't disturb us too much. It was as though they were embarrassed that there was nothing more they could do. Medicine had failed. They put us into a private ward for their benefit as much as ours.

'Emily changed. She stopped asking about when we would be going home. There was a strange sort of a peace in that little room. Sometimes she would chat with me, or ask me to sing her little bedtime songs and other times she'd be staring up at the corner of the ceiling as though she was mesmerized by what she was seeing. She started to talk to people who weren't there. She told me about how beautiful they were and the journey that she would be taking. I could see her excitement. There was no fear in her. And that gave me great comfort.

'I won't lie to you and say that I wasn't begging God for a miracle. Once Emily was diagnosed with leukaemia I prayed harder than I'd ever prayed before. I tried to bargain with God. And when that didn't work, I told him exactly how much I hated him for giving my baby such a terrible disease. I would have given my life for her. The last thing I ever expected to have to do was to sit and watch my little girl die. But despite all of that, despite all of my feelings, even I could feel the peace in that room.

'There was a particularly nice nurse who would often look in on us, even after her shift. Her name was Fiona. I think she knew I was alone. She was a kind girl. Sometimes she would sit with Emily while I went and tried to force myself to eat something in the cafeteria. Emily told her about her visions. Fiona said she'd known lots of patients who had had similar visions in the days before they passed over. Some thought the angels were coming for them. It was as if they were getting a glimpse of the other side.

'The hard part was knowing that I couldn't protect my daughter from what was happening. I felt so powerless. My daughter was slipping out of my hands and it scared me to know that, wherever it was she was going, I would not be there to take care of her. I wanted to believe that Emily was going to a better place, where she would be protected and free of pain. I was desperate for a sign.

'The end came on a Monday morning. I hadn't slept all night. Emily had been slipping in and out of consciousness all weekend. Fiona came and sat with me. I can still remember the sound of the rain on the window. It was just like the weather we have today.

'When Emily opened her eyes, we were so surprised. She looked so relaxed and happy. There was a glow about her. She told me that she would be leaving soon with her friends. She told me she was going to a beautiful place. I told her that I loved her. And then she closed her eyes.

'It was Fiona who suggested that I lie next to Emily. We could hear her breathing was becoming labored. I knew it was time. As she took her last breath I held her to me so tight, never wanting to let go.

'And just then, as the life left her body I actually felt her spirit move through me. Words don't do justice to the profound experience that it was. But I swear I could feel my daughter's soul move through me. It was the sign I had begged for. I knew my daughter was no longer in the body that I held. She had gone off on her journey, as she knew she would.

'Fiona said she had never before known such peace. When she found a long white feather under the bed she said it was a calling card from the angels.'

Ann took her cue from Anita and allowed no tears to flow. She noticed that they could now clearly see the Manhattan skyline.

'Your faith and your experience must have been a great comfort to you,' said Ann.

Anita turned to Ann and smiled. 'Sadly, I am not a saint. I'm just a selfish woman. And grief is very selfish, but it's also very human. I know my daughter lives on, but I am weak enough to want her here with me. I miss her every day. I want her here in this world but I know that I will have to settle for waiting until I see her in the next.

'I've come to believe that everything in this world happens for a reason,' said Anita. 'My Nan used to say that we all have our crosses to bear in this life. Sometimes we learn most from the very worst things. Terrible experiences can reveal great truths. I know I'll see Emily again one day.'

'I know you will too,' said Ann as she squeezed her hand.

Chapter 16

Fred's funeral was not a military affair. Norah decided that she had had quite enough of guns. She wanted to keep things simple.

Daniel had not been inside the ornate Roman Catholic church that Norah had chosen for the funeral service since Fred's wedding. His duty now was equally unfamiliar. He stared at the coffin that held the earthly remains of the best friend he had ever known and wondered why he had volunteered for pallbearer duty. The motley crew of Fred's Marine buddies who would share the sad task of carrying the coffin out of the church for the last time was gathered together in the same pew. Although none wore a uniform, the straight posture of all and the short haircuts and careful grooming of those who were still in the Corps, was ample evidence of their shared origins.

Norah had placed a photograph of Fred on top of the coffin. The image showed a smiling man, in civilian dress. Daniel guessed it was a shot that had been taken on honeymoon. Maybe Joanna had chosen the picture? She was seated next to Norah – a widow now at only thirty-three.

Daniel had forgotten how long and complicated a Catholic Mass could be, though it was something of a relief to be forced to focus on following the unfamiliar prayers and the constant need to alternately stand, sit and kneel throughout.

In the week since Fred's passing he had sought refuge in being busy. He had covered many miles of the unfamiliar Long Island landscape on his daily runs and he had helped Norah in attending to all of the administrative tasks that came with the organization of a family funeral.

He did not welcome the opportunity to reflect on his failure. If he had been more vigilant, and perhaps more forthcoming, he knew that Fred would still be alive. The anger that came with such a catastrophic failure was unfamiliar to him. The Marine

Corps had instilled in him the vital importance of leading his men home. There had been a short window of time when he had believed that the opportunity to deliver Fred to safety made sense of his experience in Fallujah.

Now nothing made sense. He wondered if it ever had. Why had he survived if this was to be the consequence?

He listened impassively as Amy attempted to eulogise her big brother. There was something pathetic and disturbing in the sight of a heavily-pregnant woman dressed in mourning clothes. The black dress that she wore stretched across her belly. Perhaps she had volunteered to deliver the eulogy because, as a lawyer, she was used to the business of public speaking. But this was not business. And in attempting to share with the congregation her memories of Fred Gallaher she was forcefully reminded of the fact that her own child would never know the unique qualities of her brother. Her baby would never have the privilege of knowing its uncle. Her sobbing, when it finally erupted, was inconsolable. The rawness of her grief tore at the heart of everyone in the church. As her husband led her back to her seat, it was the priest who stepped forward to complete the reading of the eulogy.

Daniel knew he could not face Amy, Joanna, or Norah after the funeral service. He had to fight every instinct in his body to stop himself from running from the cemetery. But instead he watched as Norah placed rosary beads on Fred's coffin before it was lowered into the cold ground.

It was Thomas Davidson, a huge hulk of a Staff Sergeant in Quantico, who suggested that they find a bar. Davidson looked uncomfortable in civilian dress. His compact hire car looked too small to accommodate his massive bulk. The front passenger seat was already occupied. Daniel had squeezed into the back seat before he realized that it was Robert Walton who was riding shotgun. The three men, somehow contained in the confines of the Japanese car, said little as they drove the five miles back to Davidson's hotel.

The dimly-lit hotel bar was empty of customers. Davidson ordered a round of beers and led the others to a corner booth. Daniel, desperate for a drink, had almost taken his first gulp when Robert raised his beer in a toast.

'Well, Semper fucking Fi,' said Robert, 'another fine man gone. Another life wasted.'

'Shut your mouth Walton,' said Thomas Davidson.

'To Fred Gallaher,' said Daniel. 'The best friend I've ever known.'

They sank their beers quickly. Another round was ordered before anyone spoke again.

'What exactly happened?' asked Thomas with uncharacteristic tenderness.

Daniel hesitated, not knowing where to begin.

'What do you *think* happened?' asked Robert. 'Or haven't you noticed the number of Marines who are abandoned by the Corps when they really need some help?'

Thomas put his face menacingly close to Robert's.

'I find it hard to believe that you were ever worthy of wearing the uniform of a Marine, Walton,' he said.

Daniel moved quickly to diffuse the situation.

'Robert served with me in Fallujah. He was a great Marine,' said Daniel. 'But he's right about the Corps. They did abandon him. The VA was too busy and too slow. But that's not what killed him. If you really want someone to blame for Fred's death then you don't need to look any further than me. Fred would still be alive today if I had been more vigilant.'

'You can't blame yourself,' said Robert. 'That sandbox messes people up.'

'He told me some stories…' said Daniel. 'I think maybe Fred just passed some kind of limit on horror. All those kills and bodies started showing up in his dreams. I guess he never really escaped.'

Thomas broke the silence.

'Every time I send a unit of new recruits out there I ask myself the same question – "Did I give them my all?". I know what they've got to face. It's bigger than some of us,' he said. 'But if there's one thing I know for sure Daniel, it's this – you gave Fred your all.

'The deployments are too long, the breaks between tours are too short and the recruits are too damn young. It's a miracle that more Marines aren't coming home with PTSD. I've seen messed-up Marines thrown into the brig when what they really need is a hospital. But things are changing.'

'Don't kid yourself,' said Robert. 'They're just cannon-fodder – pure and simple – easy to replace and almost impossible to fix. There was a time when I would have died for the Corps. I'm just glad I got out when I did.'

'Not everyone can cut it,' said Thomas.

'Man, you're so brainwashed you don't even know how to think for yourself any more,' said Robert.

'I think I've heard enough of this shit,' said Thomas. 'If you'll excuse me Daniel, I have some calls to make.'

Thomas patted Daniel on the shoulder and marched out of the bar.

'You've changed,' said Daniel.

'I've learned how to think for myself,' said Robert. 'We were all just boys when we joined up. Stick around too long and you wind up just like Davidson. I bet he doesn't have an opinion that wasn't issued to him.'

'He's a good man,' said Daniel. 'Life is a lot more complicated than any of us ever imagined when we were recruits.'

'Tell me about it,' said Robert, 'you come too close to death too many times and it changes who you are.'

'What happened to you?' asked Daniel.

'I woke up,' said Robert. 'Literally – one day I just woke up and I wondered what I knew for sure. You know, if I took a bullet; what was it that life had taught me? How had I wound up in some son-of-a-bitch desert, fighting a war I didn't even believe in, with Marines who were almost young enough to be my kids?

'I decided to stop letting other people do my thinking for me. I got tired of being a puppet. I wanted to use my mind, make up for all the years I'd let the Corps do my thinking for me. I had a lot of making up to do... For a while I thought about going back to college. But I'd had enough of being surrounded by kids the whole time. So I gave myself permission to be happy. And when it comes right down to it I realized that I'm happiest when I'm fishing and when I'm learning. So that's what I do. I spend my days on my boat now and if there's not a rod in my hand then you can bet your ass there's a book in it.

'I educate myself, feed myself and enjoy my life.'

'Your life sounds like one long vacation,' said Daniel.

'Anything is possible when you change your thinking,' said Robert. 'Why, are you jealous?'

'Confused,' said Daniel, he paused before continuing.

'You know, Fred just couldn't understand why he had survived the war when so many in his unit had died. And I completely understood what he meant. We all came close to death. We all saw a lot of death...

'Something happened to me when I went back to Fallujah and I'm not sure how to make sense of it, you know? When I was taking care of Fred I really believed that I had been saved for a reason. Now I don't know.'

'There are a lot of Freds out there,' said Robert.

'What do you mean?' asked Daniel.

'It's like you said. When you've seen so many die isn't it your duty to live the best life that you can imagine? I don't feel guilty to still be alive. I carry the memory of all of those men with me every minute of the day – but it's not a burden, it's a responsibility.

'I would not be honoring the memory of all those who fell if I lived a half-life. And maybe my life is simple now, maybe it looks selfish, but it's a happiness that I carved out of my experience. And whatever people like Davidson may think, I loved the Corps, I loved my brothers. That's why I refuse to live the rest of my life as an apology for my survival. Who would that serve?

'Crying into your beer won't bring Fred back,' said Robert, 'it won't bring anybody back. There's something seriously fucked in the world when more of our men choose to die when they come home than die in theatre. So yeah, there are plenty more guys like Fred. And if there's something more that you feel that you could have done to save Fred from himself then there are lots of men who need what you have to offer. So go ahead and use Fred's story, use your own story – do whatever it takes to create your own miracle.'

Chapter 17

It was Stephen's idea to celebrate Ann's return to Manhattan with a dinner party.

He had always been something of a salon intellectual; gathering the smartest and most interesting people in New York society for private dinners had long been a passion of his. The only dull dinner parties that Ann and Stephen had ever been forced to suffer through had invariably been work-related events or obligatory family gatherings. Seeing Stephen's excitement at the prospect of organizing a dinner in her honor was a reminder to Ann not only of her husband's goodness, but also of the fact that her accident and long recovery had caused him to suffer. He clearly missed the stimulation and shared exchange that came from these gatherings.

So, despite the fact that Ann feared that she had neither the energy nor the confidence for an evening of witty banter, she told Stephen to go ahead.

The fact was, Stephen had chosen to see her return as a pleasant surprise and not as a gesture of defiance. To him it signalled her return to normal life.

Ann did nothing to correct this idea. The promise of a return to their old life was important to Stephen. Besides, Ann was too consumed with the business of adjusting to city life to think too far ahead. Confrontation would serve no useful purpose.

She missed the safety and seclusion of their home in the Hamptons more than anyone could have imagined. It was a sign, she thought, that she had gathered her courage to leave just in the nick of time. Although their Central Park West apartment was of massive proportions (some Manhattanites lived in apartments no bigger than her closet), it still felt claustrophobic. So despite the fact that the smothering denseness of the city overwhelmed her, it equally forced her outdoors, beyond the sanctuary of the apartment and outside into Central Park.

She needed the exercise, but not nearly as much as she needed the escape. She was just grateful for the fact that the cold spring weather allowed her to hide behind a large coat and hat. It was Stephen who accompanied her on the first of these journeys. With her hand in his, protecting her from the hazards of the New York traffic as they crossed into the park, she had felt protected. Those first walks had a romantic quality that distracted her from her sense of panic and unreality. They also gave her the confidence to make the trip alone.

While Stephen was busy with work she often sought refuge in walking. Visits to the park became central to her physical rehabilitation and essential to her mental health.

New York was a city of walkers. Ann had regularly joined in the torrent of people on the city's sidewalks – glad to blend in, largely unnoticed, and relieved to be free of the gridlocked traffic. But walking before the accident had always had a purpose. It had taken her from point A to point B, enabling her to keep to a busy schedule with greatest efficiency. Before the accident she had travelled with a purpose. She had rarely taken the time to really examine her surroundings.

Meditation was something she had tried many years before. A charismatic yoga teacher had convinced her of the benefits. But Ann had quickly become bored of trying. Her busy mind proved impossible to empty, and she had soon found a more efficient use of her time. It was strange how so many years later she was reminded of those frustrating attempts to find inner peace.

As she carefully made her way beneath a freezing canopy of trees, Ann felt closer to that sense of prayerful oblivion that had once evaded her. As she gave her attention over to the beauty of life in the Park, she felt her awareness increasing. Sometimes she would stop and close her eyes to savor something of the magnificence that could, so easily, have gone unnoticed. Even then, as her focus moved to the sounds of the strollers and bikes that passed her, the beat of some faraway music and the distant hum of traffic, she felt beautifully connected to everything and everyone around her. She had stumbled upon the bliss of living consciously in the moment.

However the peace of her walks was only ever a temporary reprieve. Somehow, the enlightenment that was hers as she walked in the park quickly evaded her as she made her way back to the apartment.

With each step that she took towards her home, her ability to live in the moment deserted her. Her mind quickly filled with worries for the future. There was only so long that she could avoid Katherine. The dinner party was fast approaching. Stephen was in love with a woman who probably no longer existed.

The overwhelming fear that the cost of her newfound consciousness would leave her with nothing of her life as it had existed before the accident tore at her heart. She had returned in the hope of finding answers to these questions, but as yet, she had found none.

The morning of the dinner party brought a fresh blow. Paparazzi had scored some shots of Ann in the park. When Ann examined the pictures in a tabloid magazine that Stephen had brought to her attention (he felt she needed to know) she had been shocked by the tired and pale-looking woman they depicted and yet, equally surprised that she cared. She knew enough about the reality of image-making to understand that without a team of make-up artists and the benefit of airbrushing, she looked like any other mortal. She knew that tabloids traded on these images that ran counter to the public's perception of celebrities and the lie of perfection. Still it hurt. It felt like a violation. The experience was enough to propel her into taking extra time and care in getting ready for the dinner party.

Effortless chic was a misnomer. She had asked Georgie to arrive before the other guests. Georgie Patterson was Ann's oldest friend. They had met in the early days of their careers;

Ann as a trainee TV journalist and Georgie then a young producer. Graveyard shifts and youthful ambition had thrown them together. Although successful career progression had separated them in the workplace, they remained bound in friendship. Their relationship had survived doomed romances, fertility treatments (Georgie) and divorce (also Georgie). In the backbiting business of television, Ann knew she could always trust Georgie. It was Georgie who had been her cheerleader throughout her recovery. Though her work schedule had kept her mostly in the city, she had regularly swooped in to liberate Ann from her Mom's clutches. Stories of Georgie's eventful love life and her exuberant gossip had provided a vital lifeline to Ann. Her visits had always been a welcome distraction and a reassuring constancy at a time when everything was changing.

Georgie's presence and the chatter that came with her had an immediate calming effect on Ann. She wanted details on the guest list, though Ann knew what she really wanted to know was whether Richard was coming or not, and more importantly, who he would be bringing. Richard, a friend of Stephen's and a wealthy Internet entrepreneur, had had a brief romance with Georgie the year before. Once Georgie heard the news that Richard was bringing his latest girlfriend – a Broadway leading-lady who was only half their age – she quickly joined Ann at her industrially lit mirror to check on her make-up. As Ann dressed, Georgie brought her up-to-date with news of her latest love, a surgeon. Dr Matthew Fielding was, according to Georgie, unlike any man that she had ever dated. Ann would meet him for the first time over dinner. She wondered if Dr Fielding was feeling as nervous as she was.

Lucas Reiner announced his early arrival with an impromptu performance of Rachmaninov's piano concerto No 2. The famed pianist often expressed pity for the grand piano that went unused in Stephen and Ann's apartment. He would regularly intervene with a performance, but only, he insisted, to remind the piano of its true nature. He could rarely be charmed into playing, protesting that he was not a performing monkey, although he had sent Ann a recording of this, her favourite concerto, when she was in hospital.

'Music heals' his note had simply read. And as Ann and Georgie rushed to greet Lucas and his wife, Dorothy, a retired professor of economics from NYU, she was reminded of the feeling of childish disloyalty that was always hers whenever she embraced Dorothy Reiner. She could never help but feel the wish that Dorothy was her mother. The portly, left-leaning intellectual was the antithesis of Moira Richards. She exuded maternal warmth. It was a quality that had probably cast her as an imagined ideal mother in the minds of many.

Richard and Ava arrived soon after, as if beckoned by the music. As usual, Richard wore his uniform of sneakers and jeans, but Ava more than compensated for his lack of grooming and glamor. Her youth and beauty gave her licence to make a fashion statement in her figure-hugging dress. No matter what romantic entanglements may have complicated her introduction to the group, Ann could see that she would be a popular guest.

Mathilde was another matter entirely. Stephen's long friendship with her husband, the renowned architect Francis Forbes, had necessitated Mathilde's presence at many of these gatherings over the years. Ann's attempts at making Mathilde feel welcome had only ever succeeded in widening the divide between the two women. The French / Canadian writer, who specialized in writing short works of literary fiction that, Ann suspected, were prized chiefly for their inaccessibility, barely concealed her contempt for Ann's need-to-please. As Mathilde surveyed the other guests Ann could not help but feel that all were being judged and found to be wanting.

Nonetheless, as they sat to begin their meal Ann felt grateful to be among friends. She had successfully guarded the seat that was immediately to her right for Matthew Fielding's late arrival.

Despite the fact that this had left her seated next to Francis and Mathilde Forbes, while she could only watch as Stephen's end of the table was captivated by the dazzling Ava, she was thankful not to be the centre of attention, and glad to have the opportunity to get to know Georgie's latest love.

On first impression, Matthew Fielding was the polar-opposite of any of Georgie's many ex-lovers. The man could not be described as handsome. While his frame was athletic and slim, his hair was receding and the dissymmetry of his face was, unfortunately, offset by a sharp nose. But his smile was genuine.

And his voice had a velvet softness that would have worked on radio and must have added a soothing quality to his bedside manner. He had come straight from surgery, though he shared this fact by way of an apology and not a boast. It took some coaxing on Ann's part to learn that he was a leading cardiothoracic surgeon.

Francis saw this admission as an invitation to talk about his own recent bypass surgery and to seek his opinion of the statin medications that had been a feature of his life ever since. Matthew was sympathetic and almost managed to conceal his disappointment at being made subject to a consultation in a social setting. Ann guessed it was an inevitable downside to being a successful doctor, but one which he handled graciously.

It was Mathilde Forbes who, with a level of insensitivity that Ann had come to expect, brought the talk round to the subject of death. She was inquisitive about his emotional response to the loss of a patient in surgery. Clearly, she thought this information might provide a useful insight for one of her many bleak works of fiction.

Matthew Fielding patiently answered her questions. He spoke with a wonder and reverence for human biology that left no room for Mathilde's existential angst.

'Imagine,' he said, 'that 500,000 of our cells die each second. Each day approximately 50 billion of our cells are replaced. And each year about 98% of the molecules and atoms in our body are replaced, leaving us with a new body every year. But none of us would point to a picture of ourselves taken a year ago, or at seven years of age, or even at our birth, and mourn for the person who is lost. Our body is in a constant state of death and rebirth, but it never causes any of us to wonder if we are anything other than the person we were from our first day of our life.'

'Quite,' said Mathilde, enjoying the intellectual challenge, 'because there is a big difference between cell death and body death.'

'But it begs the question,' said Matthew, '*are* we our bodies or do we each *have* a body?'

'What do you say, Dr Fielding?' asked Mathilde.

'When you're dead, you're dead,' said Francis taking a huge slug of red wine.

'Isn't this all a little morbid?' protested Georgie, placing her hand on Matthew's.

Matthew took this as a cue to look to Ann for permission to proceed. Ann smiled in response.

'I'm fascinated,' she said.

'The fact is,' said Matthew, 'death is not a specific moment in the way you generally see on television. It's a process that begins when the heart stops beating, the lungs stop breathing and the brain function ends. During a cardiac arrest, all of these criteria are present. But that doesn't stop us from using emergency medicine to attempt to re-start the heart. And sometimes we succeed, though not nearly as often as medical dramas would have you believe. So during the seconds or minutes it might take you to revive a patient, when the heart, lungs and brain have all ceased functioning, what are they, if not dead?'

'My Mom warned me that some doctors have God complexes,' said Georgie, winking.

Francis fiddled uncharacteristically with the collar of his turtleneck.

'It's impossible to be dead one moment and then alive the next,' said Mathilde. 'Clearly the medical definition of death is the problem here. Nobody survives death.'

'People survive the clinical definition of death every day in emergency rooms and operating theatres across the country,' Matthew replied. 'But what really interests me is the proof of consciousness that some of those patients report while the brain has absolutely ceased functioning.'

'Proof? Of consciousness?' asked Mathilde, looking incredulous.

'Absolutely,' said Matthew, 'some patients report spiritual experiences that I am in no position to substantiate, but a fascinating minority can accurately report medical procedures and conversations that have taken place when they have been brain dead.'

'Perhaps they have simply watched too many medical dramas?' said Mathilde.

'The instruments and procedures that we use in real hospitals bear little relationship to anything that you'd see on television,' said Matthew. 'I have heard enough compelling evidence from patients and colleagues to believe that consciousness survives clinical death. Certainly, I believe that in the near future, the current narrow scientific concept that the brain is the source of consciousness will be proved to be incorrect. Biology, like all branches of science has been guilty of perpetuating a mechanistic view of reality. That approach has been necessary until now and it has certainly been very useful...'

'Right,' said Francis, 'it's trained our surgeons and created our medicines. It's saved the lives of more than one of us at this table.'

'Absolutely,' said Matthew enthusiastically. 'But each of us knows that we are all so much more than a bundle of cells. We are not simply biological machines. Science needs to evolve if we are to answer some of the most compelling questions like – what happens when we die?'

'But isn't it something of a quantum leap to suggest that science should seek to provide answers to what are, essentially, matters of faith and superstition? Particularly when you base your argument on the subjective experiences of a handful of patients,' asked Mathilde.

'Well, think about it,' said Matthew, 'even if only one of those experiences is true, then that changes everything. If we could prove only a handful of incidents where consciousness survived clinical death, than that would be enough to turn our understanding of biology on its head.

'Besides, a quantum leap really is nothing of the impossible magnitude that our vernacular usually implies. It is a wonderous and inexplicable shift that challenges many of our assumptions about the world and how it works.

'Science has so many more questions to answer – that's what makes it so exciting. And I truly believe that we are about to experience a shift in many of our ideas about consciousness and the brain. Because right now, we just don't have all the answers. And I find that pretty exciting.'

Mathilde quickly steered the conversation to an area that allowed her to more easily display her intellect and experience, but Ann remained locked in the words that Matthew had spoken.

As the dinner party continued she felt almost drunk with excitement that her experience had not placed her entirely beyond the range of rational thought and understanding and dinner party conversation.

Chapter 18

Robert was right. There were many more like Fred, who thought that suicide would allow them to escape themselves and their pain. Some sort of evil had infected so many of those who had served in Iraq. The horror of what they had witnessed and what they had done had traveled home with them, gnawing at their minds, contaminating their feelings and strangling their attempts to ever really leave the sandbox. They were sick, not weak. The source of their contaminant was in the past, but it pervaded their daily lives and it threatened their futures. The past could not be undone, Daniel knew that, but still he wondered at the possibilities.

He had been trawling for information online when he stumbled across the research that was to confirm the truth of his instincts. When he read the report that those who experienced a near-death experience while attempting suicide were at practically no risk of ever making another suicide attempt again, he knew that he had struck gold. The reported fact that learning about a near-death experience could have many of the same suicide-prevention effects as having the experience, sent Daniel's mood and imagination soaring.

His experience was not unique. What he had only recently considered to be a shameful secret had the potential to spread, like some benevolent virus, infecting all who needed it with hope. He had risked his life so many times before to save the lives of his fellow Marines. Could he allow the risk of ridicule to stop him from this mission?

Without pausing to consider the answer to that question, Daniel set about his work.

Daniel posted an open invitation to near-death survivors who were willing to share their stories on camera before he had time to lose his nerve or to doubt in his abilities. It was only when the replies began to fill up his in-box that he wondered how someone with his lack of experience in interviewing and operating a camera could hope to pull off such an ambitious project.

It was a newfound sense of purpose and thoughts of Fred that propelled him past those initial fears. Though, in retrospect, he realized that he had been blessed in his selection of his first interview subject. Josephine Robert had been a natural story-teller.

It was a granddaughter of Josephine's who had contacted Daniel, so he knew little of her story when he had first arrived at the assisted living facility outside Bangor that was her home. The hospital smell that greeted him at the reception desk only added to his nerves.

'Miss Josephine has a visitor!' cheered a nurse from behind the desk.

Daniel signed the visitor's book, relieved to find that his host was happy to conduct an enthusiastic monolog. Years of working with the elderly had clearly left the nurse unable to speak at a normal volume. She spoke at something approaching a shout with a patronizing choice of words that she most probably intended as a kindness to her patients. Daniel suspected she was more suited to working with small children than frail and aging adults.

'Miss Josephine has refused her medication this morning,' said the nurse as she led him down a hallway dotted with walkers and wheelchairs. 'She's a stubborn one, for sure. She wouldn't be told that she'll pay for that poor choice later on this afternoon. She said she didn't want to be sleepy while she was being interviewed. I told her it was all the same if it was Barbara Walters coming to film her; she needs to take her painkillers. That arthritis of hers isn't going to thank her for it. Still what can you do?'

They stopped outside one of the many identikit doors, which

the nurse opened without knocking.

'Here we are,' said the nurse. 'Try not to keep her too long. She tries to fight it, but the fact is that she does get tired. Miss Josephine your visitor is here.'

Josephine's tiny frame was almost consumed by the armchair where she sat. A blanket covered her legs. When Daniel shook her hand, he held it with the same tenderness that a baby bird would have demanded. Josephine did not release her hand from his until she had taken the opportunity to carefully examine his face. She nodded her approval.

The nurse quickly left them alone.

'So you are the one who is gathering these stories of death?' she said.

Daniel nodded as he quickly moved to set up the video camera on a tripod.

'It's a good thing that you do,' she said. 'Stories have the power to teach so many lessons, it's important to pass them on. It is our duty.'

The video camera was running.

'Would you like to tell your story now?' asked Daniel.

Josephine took a deep breath and closed her eyes. When she opened them again she smiled.

'I grew up in another world. It's hard for my children and my grandchildren to understand. So much has changed. I am 88 years old now, soon I will be gone. But death holds no fear for me.

'A great truth was revealed to me a long, long time ago. And though I was only a girl of ten years old when I learned this truth, it has never left me. My memory of it is still fresh and true.

'My home was a place of shame and fear. Though my Mother never spoke of it, it is impossible for a Mother to conceal these feelings from a child. It was not until the death of my Father and the arrival of my Grandmother that I began to understand the source of my Mother's anxiety. I was six years old when my Grandmother came to live with us. She told me that we belonged to the Abenaki tribe. This confused me greatly – my Mother had always insisted that we were French-Canadian. My name, after all, was Josephine. But I never doubted my Grandmother's word. I knew I was different from the other kids, no matter how much my Mother tried to pretend that I was not. And when my Mother and my Grandmother spoke harsh words to one another, they spoke in a language that I did not understand, but that I knew was not French.

'There were many reasons, my Grandmother explained, why my Mother wanted me to know nothing of my Abenaki heritage. At that time it was a dangerous thing to be Abenaki. This wasn't something that I truly understood until I was much older and I read about the 'Perkins Project' of that time. I understood then why my mother had fled Vermont with my father. Many Abenaki people were subjected to sterilizations in the name of eugenics. Others had children taken away from them. There were many frightening Ku Klux Klan rallies. It's hard to believe that such things happened on American soil in my lifetime, but it is the truth. Just because something may be hard to believe does not make it any less true.

'So my mother's fears were well-founded. But all this meant to me as a child was the realization that I could not share the many stories that my Grandmother told me while my mother worked in the mill. Those stories were a wonderful secret that bound us one to the other.

'While my mother worked my Grandmother filled my head with tales of Gluskabe, of Pamola and of the shaman who could transform himself into animal form. My mother took me to Mass and taught me about Jesus while my Grandmother insisted that all was a great mystery. Grandmother believed that everything was alive and must be respected. So she greeted the sun each morning and said a prayer of thanks over her first drink of water.

'Like most children, I gave these matters little thought, I saw the world through the eyes of a child. Talk of death and Heaven seemed like some faraway land.

'But all of that changed when I was making my way home from school one February day. There was a neighbour's boy – Billy Evans was his name – he used to follow me along the track that led to our homes. His father was a cruel man, he had a reputation for making trouble in the town. Now I can see that Billy must have suffered greatly at the hands of his father in order to have become the cruel bully that he was. But as a ten-year-old girl I was not aware of this. Billy scared me. When he threw stones at me and called me names like 'river rat' and 'gypsy', I was afraid.

'Most days I ran home as fast as I could, just to avoid that boy. On this particular February day I was in a great rush. I must have been a mile from home when I rounded a sharp bend by the woods and saw a malamute standing there, right in the middle of the path. It stopped me in my tracks.

'Even though it looked just like a wolf, I was not afraid. Grandmother had told me so many stories about those dogs and I understood them to be a friend of the Abenaki people. There was an instant connection between us. I walked slowly towards the malamute, extending my closed hand so as to offer him my scent. There was something majestic and familiar about the animal. His beauty and calm, just standing there in the melting snow, is something that I picture clearly to this day. I wondered if this was a shaman who had taken the form of an animal? But just as I was about to pat the malamute, there was a noise from behind the bend. I knew instantly that Billy Evans was chasing after me. When the malamute disappeared into the woods in a flash of grey, it seemed like instinct to follow after him.

'I followed his prints in the snow. I could hear him charging through the undergrowth. There were glimpses of him as I continued deeper into the woods. When I finally emerged on the banks of a stream I saw him standing, tantalizingly close, on the other side of the water.

'If I had been thinking clearly I would never have attempted to cross at that point. A thaw was setting in and the waters were more swollen that usual. But excitement and curiosity got the better of me. I was in the middle of the river when I lost my footing on a slippery rock.

'The coldness of the water was a great shock. And the strength of the current was too strong for me. Even a strong swimmer would have struggled to survive. I was tossed and turned, numbed to the iciness of the water. Pain was quickly replaced by a calm sleepiness.

'Immediately I saw something that was beyond my experience. I became an observer of the scene. Instead of being in the water, I was above the water. While I watched my small body being swept downstream I was unconcerned. There was no fear. Instead there was a profound remembering that I had returned to myself – almost as if I had woken up from a dream.

'The appearance of a bright form beside me did not frighten me. When I turned my attention to this form I saw that it was Jesus and I was filled with a huge rush of love. Suddenly it was as if everything around me was pulsating with love.

'This life force of loving energy ran through everything – the trees, the birds in the trees, even the water. It was as if everything had been made manifest by this love. Everything was so clearly connected in this great and living love that I wondered how I could ever have forgotten it was so, but even as that thought occurred to me, I realized that my true self, my eternal self, had always known this to be true. My mother and my Grandmother had both been leading me toward this truth. Everything was alive and everything was connected, just as my Grandmother had always insisted.

'I was exhilarated and curious. I asked Jesus if he had come to take me home. Though I spoke only with my thoughts. When he told me it was not my time, I flew into a terrible tantrum. I could not bear the idea of being removed from that profound love.

Jesus responded to my display of bad manners like a bemused parent.

'His last gift to me that day was to share with me the living beauty of the Earth. As He lifted me higher and higher, I could see more and more beauty. In one great rush I could see all of Pittsfield, then all of Maine, then all of the east coast, until I could see the whole and complete beauty of the Earth. It was not until many years later, when man first travelled to the moon, that I saw a similar sight. Though the image I saw on my old TV set did not compare to the pulsating and loving vision of the Earth that Jesus shared with me.

'My adventure in death came to an end in a blinding flash of light. When I awoke I was lying in a hospital bed, with my mother and my Grandmother both by my side. They told me that my body had been pulled from the river in town. I was so cold they were certain I had died. But a doctor in the hospital insisted that I be warmed. He saved my life.'

For the first time since she had begun to speak, Josephine looked directly at Daniel.

'You too know the truth?' she asked.

Daniel nodded.

'It changes a person,' she said.

'I have told my story many times to many people. Most of them think I'm a crazy old Indian woman. But I don't worry about that. It is not my job to change their minds. I simply speak the truth. Not everyone is prepared to consider the true mystery of our life. Many choose to sleepwalk through their lives, pretending to themselves that they will never face death.

'I will face death again soon, and all I can tell you is this; I have no fear. My spirit will, I know, be released into a love that is beyond all imagination. It is my sincerest hope that I have used my time on Earth wisely and that others will take hope from my story.'

Chapter 19

Synchronicity was not a concept that Ann would have subscribed to before her accident, but suddenly she saw evidence of it everywhere. Matthew Fielding had been delivered to her side on the night of the dinner party for a particular purpose; she saw that now. It was not some random act of the Universe that had caused Anita to share the story of her daughter's death. Everything was happening as it was supposed to. Ann did not need to fight against the current of change that had swept through her life since her brush with death.

Everything was beginning to make sense. People and events were conspiring to validate the truth of her experience.

She felt brilliantly and giddily liberated from any fears for her own sanity. It must have been the physical pain of her injuries that had made her yearn for a return to the person she had been before the accident.

The pain and the near-constant presence of her mother had confused her thinking; the combination of those two potent forces had obscured from her the joy of her experience.

After the party she had made love to Stephen with a passion that was transcendental. No words were needed. She had realized that there was no need to fear for her marriage. There was no need to fear for anything.

Once liberated from death, the notion of fear was completely false and delusional. The French had an expression for orgasm that she had never understood, 'la petite mort', the little death. But that too made sense to her.

Her connection to Stephen had been heightened by her awareness of the now; there was no past and no future, only the pure truth of that moment. She had indeed died to everything but the beauty of that present moment. And in that moment of total and wondrous awareness she saw the depth of her love reflected perfectly back in Stephen and she felt connected to him as she had never before felt.

It was almost painful to recall that her ideas about love had once been so limited and conditional. She had been more like her Mom than she could ever before have realized. Like Moira Richards, she too had held herself back from those around her, playing life like it was a game that some would win and some would lose. But there was no need to place a limit on love, it was an infinite resource that was totally non-hazardous. Withholding love had punished no one but herself. Her love for Stephen was without condition. When she really thought about it, she even loved her mother.

She was high on life.

There was no going back. She wondered how she could ever have wanted to undo her experience.

The feeling stayed with her the next morning. She held her first cup of coffee in her hands and was conscious of the gratitude she felt for the warmth of the mug in her hands and the taste of that first sip.

All around her she noticed blessings in the mundane things of life that had once gone unnoticed; the feel of her cashmere sweater, the smell of wax on the kitchen table and the view of the park from the window.

She walked across to the park without any thought of the paparazzi shots that had appeared in the tabloids only the day before. Her attention was focused only on the now. With each step she grew more certain that happiness was a choice available to everyone, it did not necessitate a particular career or lover or bank balance. It was available to everyone in the timeless gift of living fully in the moment.

Ann felt a palpable connection to everything and everyone around her. She recognised a reflection of herself, and yes, of God, in the faces of everyone she saw. The strength of her love for these strangers was almost overwhelming. It stopped her in her tracks.

She knew then that she wanted to share her story with everyone.

Chapter 20

When he slept he dreamt of Fred. It must have been a dream, though it had felt like something closer to a visit.

Fred had stood at the foot of his bed. At first, the luminosity of his presence had obscured his identity, but once Daniel's eyes had adjusted he could clearly see that it was Fred. His hair was short again and his face was no longer distorted by pain and bloating. It was Fred all right, but somehow it was if the very essence of his best friend had been distilled of everything but love, leaving no space for fear; it was Fred at his most perfect.

David wondered if he was seeing a ghost. In the instant that the thought crossed his mind, Fred understood him and laughed.

'It's me, Danny boy,' he said.

The grief that Daniel had managed to suppress since the funeral suddenly exploded out of him.

'I'm so sorry Freddie, I failed you,' he said.

'You loved me,' said Fred, as he moved closer to Daniel. 'You loved me then and you love me still. Love never fails. I had my own lessons to learn.'

Daniel sobbed. It felt as though the intensity of his grieving had been given leave to be released. Even as he cried he could feel the weight of the burden that he had been carrying leave him. The relief was immeasurable.

'You, of all people, know better than to cry for me,' said Fred.

'I miss you Freddie,' said Daniel.

'I never left you,' said Fred.

With that, Fred reached out and touched the centre of Daniel's forehead.

The touch instantly shattered Daniel's perspective of his surroundings.

In that single moment, Daniel's illusion that he existed in a material world of inert, dead matter was replaced by a living symphony of light. He dived into an ocean of knowingness and of pure being. Waves of vibration, thought and light carried him along in a state of pure bliss. He was, at once, the observer and the observed. The living intelligence of his being transcended the illusion of separation. Fundamental to everything was the profound unity of a common source. All was love.

Time lost all meaning and power. He existed only in the now.

'You're on the right path,' said Fred. 'Tell Mom I'm sorry. I didn't know how much I would hurt her, hurt everyone... I didn't really know what I was doing. Tell her they're helping me to heal now.'

A young and beautiful woman with flowing black hair appeared next to Fred. Despite her changed appearance, Daniel knew that it was Josephine Robert. Like Fred, Josephine glowed with happiness.

'It's time to tell your story,' she said.

Chapter 21

Ann put a call through to Katherine Krukowski as soon as she returned home to the apartment. It was not an impulsive act to invite Katherine to meet her that day, but it felt crucial to use the momentum of her newfound certainty and conviction to fulfil her destiny. What was she if not a truth teller? She had become a journalist with the intention of uncovering truths and of telling stories that had the power to transform lives.

Was there ever a greater story than this? If people were made to finally understand the great lie of death then who could predict the changes that were possible, not only in the lives of individuals but in the world at large? So many of the day-to-day concerns of life (and of the world that she had previously reported) seemed petty when seen through the lens of her spiritual revelation.

There had been a purpose to Ann's experience. She was never more certain of anything before in her life. Everything had been leading up to the moment where she could tell her story. Katherine would understand. Nothing was bigger than this.

In the thirty minutes that it took Katherine to make it from the downtown offices of the news studio to the apartment, Ann did not rush to change her clothes or to gather up the evidence that she had so unsuccessfully used to try to persuade Stephen.

This time she understood the truth was within her. And so she sat peacefully – using her awareness of the beauty of each moment to gather her thoughts and to prepare to speak from her soul.

When Katherine arrived, Ann noticed that she brought with her a great deal of noise. She barked orders into the iPhone that she held to her ear, while demanding a caffeine-fix from the housekeeper and shrugging a greeting to Ann. Her attention was all over the place, everywhere and nowhere at the same time.

Ann continued to center herself as she noticed these things, and waited until the telephone conversation had ended and the tray of coffee had been delivered before asking Katherine to turn off her cell phone.

'You're kidding me, right?' said Katherine. 'I've got lawyers crawling all over a package that has to go to air tonight. I can't fall off radar just like that.'

'I need your full attention,' said Ann.

Reluctantly Katherine switched off her cell phone. She took a deep breath and settled back into her chair, all the while surveying Ann.

'You're looking a lot better now,' said Katherine.

'I've never felt better,' said Ann.

'Better enough to come back to us?'

'I believe I am,' said Ann.

'Finally,' said Katherine, beaming, 'they've been killing us in the ratings. I've been losing sleep over the May sweeps.'

'I just need you to green-light a special project that I want to focus on,' said Ann.

'Anything,' said Katherine, 'what's the subject?'

'Death,' said Ann.

'Excuse me?' said Katherine.

'I want to do a feature on the fact that life continues after death.'

'You're just messing with me, right?'

'I've never been more serious about anything in my life,' said Ann. 'What would you do if you knew that death was not the end? Wouldn't you want to share that news with everyone you knew? Isn't that the biggest story that anyone could ever break?'

Katherine dropped her head into her hands and began to massage her temples.

'Something happened to me after the accident,' said Ann.

'No kidding,' said Katherine, 'did it involve a blow to the

head?'

'I don't see any need for jokes at my expense,' said Ann.

'Frankly, I'm not entirely sure that you're not making a joke at my expense,' said Katherine. 'Help me understand here.'

Ann looked directly into Katherine's eyes.

'I died on the day of my accident,' said Ann. 'It's not something that I would ever have thought possible before this happened to me, so I can understand your surprise. But I found myself outside my body. I observed the entire scene of the accident, I even observed the rescue workers. There are witness statements that verify my account of things that happened that morning; things that happened while I was bleeding to death, trapped and unconscious in the back of my car. But none of that matters really, because it was what happened afterwards, while I was absent from my body and from this world that really altered me.

'That's the story that I need to tell, because that's when I learned that life is eternal. There is no death. There's only love.

'My eyes have been opened by this experience. I see beauty in things that I never even noticed before. I feel so connected to everything and everyone. It's wonderful.

'The idea of returning to work disturbed me. I think because I thought it would necessitate returning to the person I was before the accident. And that is something I cannot do. But now I see the experience was given to me for a reason; so I can report it! I can reach a huge audience. People trust me. I mean, who out there has never asked the question, 'what happens when we die?' Death is something we all have to face sometime. And now I have the experience to help answer that question. This will be the most important story of my life.

'It's risky, I know, but I have to believe that the truth will set me free,' said Ann.

Katherine's jaw slackened unattractively in disbelief.

'So let's make sure I've got this straight,' said Katherine. 'You want me to help you commit professional suicide?'

'You think it's professional suicide to tell the truth?' said Ann.

'I don't think,' said Katherine, 'I know! And if you were really thinking clearly, you'd know it too.

'Besides, even if you really think this is true for you that doesn't make it true for everybody else. We are in the business of reporting the news. Our stories are objective, accurate and verifiable. Politics, war, terrorism, technology, natural disasters; all fact-based reports. Facts are fundamental to what we do. There can be no truth without evidence to support it.

'Matters of faith are entirely personal and subjective. We leave those questions to the private religious practices of individuals. They are not up for discussion on our news show or on any news show. You know that.'

'So we'll examine every facet of our existence except the one that really counts? said Ann.

'You know better than this,' said Katherine.

'Last night I met a cardio-thoracic surgeon who spoke of the survival of consciousness after clinical death,' said Ann.

'Lots of smart people believe in life after death,' said Katherine. 'Then again, plenty more don't. It's a matter of personal faith and a matter of opinion.'

'If people understood that they were eternal and loved beyond imagination, don't you think we would experience a huge shift in every area of our lives; politics, crime, war, poverty?' said Ann. 'This goes to the heart of all of those issues. Why do we insist on avoiding the topic of our spiritual life?'

'Because people are people, and people will never agree when it comes to religion,' said Katherine. 'You know that. People fly airplanes into buildings because they think their God is better than our God. People start wars because they believe their religion gives them the moral authority to murder. Religion hasn't exactly got a great record of transforming lives for the better. That's why we have to limit our reporting to the facts.'

'But I'm not talking about religion,' said Ann. 'I'm talking about what it means to be fully human. We are all of us spiritual beings, not machines. If we could come to terms with what death really means then I truly believe we would lead more conscious lives.'

Katherine sighed.

'I'm sure that in a perfect world there might be some logic to your argument,' she said. 'But we don't live in a perfect world. And it's not your job to convert people to your point of view. We don't do God. We just don't.

'Even if I was foolish enough to allow you to broadcast your views, have you given any thought to the consequences for your career? No-one would ever take you seriously again.'

'That's a chance I'm willing to take,' said Ann.

'Then I'm sorry to hear that,' said Katherine, 'because if you were thinking rationally you would never say that.'

Katherine stood up to leave.

'You need more time to recover. Right now I'd say you need protecting from yourself. A therapist could help.

'Maybe I'm guilty of putting you under too much pressure to rush back to the show. Viewers miss you. We all miss you, really. But you're not ready to come back. And you won't be able to come back until you're thinking clearly.

'Please get all the help you need. And in the meantime don't repeat any of the things you've said to me this morning unless you're talking to someone you can trust one hundred per cent.'

Katherine turned on her iPhone.

'I'll see myself out,' she said.

Chapter 22

Norah didn't touch his face.

She kept her distance. The hug when she greeted Daniel at the door was perfunctory. She had escaped his arms before their embrace had been allowed to stray beyond the normal boundaries of politeness and into the realms of friendship or consolation. While Daniel took a seat at the kitchen table, Norah busied herself with the coffee pot. She turned only to clean the already pristine table and then kept her eyes firmly on the surface. When she spoke to him she wiped with even greater vigour than before.

'You drove all the way down from Maine, huh?' she said.

'Yeah,' said Daniel. 'I need to talk to you.'

He placed his hand on top of hers for the briefest of moments, until she snatched it away. She quickly exchanged her washcloth for the coffee pot and poured only one cup. She placed the cup on the table, just out of Daniel's reach while she remained standing by the worktop.

'What,' she said, 'they don't have phones in Portland?'

Daniel wrapped his hands tightly around the cup of coffee.

'I'm sorry I didn't come back after the funeral,' he said. 'I wasn't even sure I'd make it through the service. But I shouldn't have left without saying goodbye.'

Norah shrugged. 'It seems to be the style, doesn't it, for you boys to leave without saying goodbye?'

'You have every reason to be angry,' said Daniel.

'I'm not angry,' said Norah as she threw down the washcloth. 'The fact is, I'm not anything. There's nothing in here. I'm empty. Everybody looks at me with pity now, like they know how I feel; but they don't. I don't need sympathy, or flowers that make the house smell like a funeral home, or anyone showing up here to hold my hand. So really Daniel, don't waste my time.'

Daniel pushed his coffee cup away from him and paused for a long silent moment.

'I saw him,' he said.

'What?' said Norah.

'I saw Freddie,' said Daniel. 'He wanted me to come here. He wanted me to tell you that he's sorry for what he did.'

'Jesus,' said Norah, slumping slightly against the worktop.

'I know this is hard for you to believe,' said Daniel. 'But I know it wasn't just a dream. I know it was really him.'

Norah threw herself across the table and hit Daniel across the face.

'Get out of my house!' she said.

Daniel did not recoil. Instead, he held on to Norah's hands.

'Listen to me,' said Daniel, 'he made me promise to tell you that's he's sorry. He's so sorry Norah for what he did to you, for what he did to us.'

The sob that erupted from Norah surprised them both. Daniel released her hands from his grip and she fell back onto the chair next to his. She wiped the tears from her face as if to wonder at their source.

'Just tell me you're not going crazy too,' she said.

'You don't need to worry about me,' Daniel replied.

Norah did not reach for a Kleenex. She let the tears and snot flow as she eyed Daniel.

'You think I don't see him?' she said. 'He's a ghost in every corner of this house. I sleep in his sweatshirts, I sniff his after-shave and sometimes I even try to persuade myself that he's just on a tour of duty; that he'll be back. But wishing will never make it so. Daniel, he's gone. We both did everything we could to save him, but Freddie is gone.'

'I could have done more,' said Daniel.

'Nonsense,' said Norah, 'you really will drive yourself crazy if you keep replaying the whole thing over and over in your head. Trust me, I know.'

'I wasn't entirely honest with Freddie,' said Daniel. 'At the time I told myself that he didn't need to know and that he wouldn't have been able to handle the truth if I had told him; but that's not true. I didn't tell him because I was afraid.'

'What didn't you tell him Daniel?' asked Norah, reaching for his hand.

Daniel ran his hand along the scar that marked his face.

'When this happened to me,' he said, 'it changed everything. I don't know why I ever went back to Fallujah in the first place. Sure, I needed the money after the divorce. But after everything I saw there before, I think I must have had some sort of deathwish. When we hit that IED my whole world ended. You can't come back from the dead and not be changed by it.'

'The trauma changed you?' asked Norah.

'The trauma we experienced there changed us all,' said Daniel. 'But that's not what I'm talking about...

'I actually died that day. By the time they got me to the field hospital, I was already gone. It was only the fact that the medics there had so much practice in piecing people back together that they even attempted to resuscitate me.'

Daniel paused.

'I've never told anyone what I experienced that day,' he said. 'But I'd like to tell you now if that's okay?'

Norah nodded.

'I never thought much about death before that day... I'd seen a lot of people die, I'd even killed people, but I never wondered about what happened when a person died. Because, to me it was obvious; death was the end. And maybe there was a bullet or a bomb with my name on it, but it was my job to do everything in my power to avoid ever meeting it. It was my mission to do whatever it took to protect myself, my brothers and whoever was in my charge. Simple as that.

'When my truck hit that IED I didn't have much time to think about anything. I wasn't wearing a helmet or a seatbelt. The force

119

of it, the noise of it and the feeling of powerlessness – knowing that if the blast didn't kill me then there would probably be a gunman to finish off the job – time seemed to slow down. And then there was just this nothing...

'At first I was conscious of only a cold darkness. It felt like I was in that void for a long time until it dawned on me that I was still thinking. And since I was still thinking, I realized that I still existed. That really surprised me. I mean, I'd never believed in God, I'd never had much time for religion. Too many years spent watching my Mom use her faith as a weapon, I suppose. She always used to tell me that I would go to Hell. And for a while I wondered if she had been right. I wondered if I was in Hell. The feeling of isolation filled me with panic, I wondered if this was all my life had been worth; if I was getting the punishment I deserved. And in my fear, I called out for help. Though I can't even tell you how I did that since I wasn't conscious of having a body.

'Immediately, a tiny spark of light became visible. The more I looked at the light, the closer I got to it, or maybe it got closer to me, I don't know. It was brighter than anything I'd ever seen before. Just looking at it made me feel loved. It made me feel worthy.

'I was so excited. Something in me recognized that I was going home. I wanted to join with the light. There was so much love, more love than I could ever have imagined. It was such a high.

'I knew the light was my source; that it was the source of all things. And that source was pure love. Everything was connected through the source. Then I realized that in my lifetime I had failed to see that connection and to feel that love. I felt a great sadness that I had not noticed such a fundamental truth – it seemed as though I had wasted a wonderful opportunity to grow and to learn.

'As soon as that thought entered my mind, I was given the option of returning to the world. The choice was mine. And I knew that I would be returning to the source again. That knowledge gave me the courage to return to my life, to this world.'

Daniel returned his gaze to Norah.

'The medics called me Lazarus. I'd been down so long they were just about to give up on me when my heart finally began to beat again.

'And here I am. Walking round with this secret – with this knowledge – but I haven't told a soul before you. I had the opportunity to tell Freddie, but I didn't take it.'

Daniel's tears erupted before he had a chance to stop them. He hid his face in his hands while Norah rubbed his hair.

'What did you want to tell Freddie?' said Norah.

Without looking up or removing his hands from his face, Daniel replied, 'I wanted to tell him that life never ends. I wanted to tell him that there is no over. We have to work through our pain and know that we are loved.'

Norah wrapped her arms around Daniel's shoulders and kissed his hair, letting her own tears run freely.

'And look what you've just done, Daniel,' she said. 'You've told me. You've told me. And I needed to hear those words more than you could ever know.'

Chapter 23

Ann knew Katherine would call Stephen. It was inevitable. She would claim concern for Ann's mental health, but really the phone call would be Katherine's underhand way of ensuring that Ann was gagged. It would be easy to appeal to Stephen sense of logic. And Ann did not want to fight with Stephen.

She wasn't running away. She just needed time alone, to think. And so she simply slipped her laptop and phone into a fashionably large purse and walked out the door of the apartment with nothing to indicate that this was anything but one of her regular therapeutic strolls to the park. But she did not go to the park. Instead, she left her Central Park West apartment building, hailed a cab and headed downtown.

It occurred to her to call Georgie, but she knew that would be the first place that Stephen would look. She needed time to think. In the end she opted for the anonymity of a large midtown hotel. Once she had made that decision she relaxed back into her seat in the yellow cab, happy to have bought herself some time.

The sight of St Patrick's Cathedral inspired a change of plan.

How many times in her life had she passed St Patrick's without a second thought? This time the peculiarly gothic creation that was dwarfed by New York's modern skyline captured her attention as soon as it came into view. It appeared as a spiritual beacon in a sea of rampant materialism. Somehow she knew she had to go there.

She stopped the cab, threw too many dollars in the direction of the driver and made her way up the steps of the cathedral as quickly as her still-frail body would allow. But whatever feeling she may have had that she had arrived for an appointment with destiny disappeared as soon as she entered the church. There was no great revelation awaiting her – only the predictable mix of shuffling tourists and worshippers. There was nothing in the cathedral on that Monday afternoon to suggest the promise of a mystical revelation.

Ann felt suddenly dizzy – overwhelmed equally by her own foolishness and the exertion of almost running up the steps. She slid into a pew at the back of the cathedral to catch her breath and to gather her thoughts.

Just what had she expected? Did she really think that God would make an appearance in Manhattan just so that everyone would know that Ann Richards was telling the truth? Would anything short of an act of biblical proportions ever hope to persuade the people in her life that she was sane and right?

She had visited many magnificent churches in Europe on her travels with Stephen. He had been in awe of the engineering and of the art, she had been drawn by the beauty of the candles and had insisted on lighting a candle in each church that they had visited, though she had never prayed.

It wasn't Stephen's teasing of her that had prevented her from enjoying some quiet moments of meditation, but her own embarrassment at the behaviour of other American tourists who had snapped photographs and talked too loudly – oblivious to the sacredness of the place to those who were praying.

In truth, she had never been able to connect with that feeling of sacredness. None of those ancient, towering monuments had ever persuaded her of the glory of God. Instead, she had viewed them as the last vestiges of the superstitious, and yes, the ignorant.

This time it felt different. She was no longer an outsider. As she regained her composure and overcame her disappointment that there would be no miracle that would return her world to its equilibrium, she discovered a sort of peace. This was a safe haven. A place where faith was not only permitted, but celebrated.

Strange to think that she had visited so many different churches in her lifetime and yet she had completely failed to appreciate the radical and alternative view of reality that faith afforded.

She wanted to light a candle.

There was a quiet alcove, away from the tourists and with only one solitary worshipper. Ann made her way towards this spot. She put a five dollar bill into the slot where the candles were dispensed and carefully lit her candle.

Although she was not a Catholic, she recognized the figure of the Blessed Mother as she serenely gazed at the glow of the candles at her feet. Ann sat back into the pew. She focussed all of her attention on the warm glow of the candlelight as she centered her thoughts on only that moment. Candles, she knew, were usually lit for some special intention. What was her intention? She allowed her mind to wander until it came back with the simple answer; peace.

Peace, peace, peace, peace. She repeated it like a mantra in her mind until there was no trace of anxiety left in her body and she finally understood that all was unfolding exactly as it should be. The feeling of acceptance was such a relief to her that she soon felt tears running down her cheeks. She rummaged in the pocket of her coat for a Kleenex, but found none.

'Need one of these?' said a kind voice.

'Thanks,' said Ann, taking the tissue from an old woman with grey hair and the sort of wrinkled skin that had become largely extinct in a Manhattan filled with dermatologists and plastic surgeons. Her black overcoat looked several sizes too big.

'I'm new to this,' said Ann.

'Crying?' said the old woman.

'No, praying,' said Ann, sniffling.

'Well, I've spent a lifetime praying and I can assure you that the crying is optional,' said the old woman.

'They're happy tears really,' said Ann.

'You don't sound so sure about that,' said the old woman. 'Before they forced me to retire, I ran a convent school, so I've heard all kinds of stories. And I'm not even sure that I believe in happy tears.'

'I guess I'm confused,' said Ann. 'And I guess I came here looking for some answers.'

'Nothing wrong with that,' said the old woman.

'I'm not even Catholic,' said Ann. 'In fact, I'm not really anything. My life was good before the accident. I wasn't aware that I was missing anything at all. But then I had my accident and I actually died. The things I saw... the things I now know to be true... well, they're not things that I can reconcile with my life as it was before. My world has turned upside down. I mean it's not like I was looking for God.'

'But He found you anyway,' said the old woman.

'Yes, He found me alright,' said Ann. 'But He didn't find my husband or my friends.'

'You're luckier than you know,' said the old lady. 'I've been a nun since the age of 19. I devoted my entire life to God, but there have been many times when my faith has waned.

'The world can be a cruel place. Sometimes it's hard to believe in a loving God. Whenever my faith was low I would turn for comfort to the writings of saints who had had mystical experiences. It comforted me to know that there were people in the world who've had a real experience of God. You see, it is one thing to have a tangible experience of God and quiet another to rely on faith alone. "Blessed are those who do not see and yet believe."

'Be patient with your husband and your friends. Give them a chance to catch up.'

She paused quietly. 'There must be some purpose to your experience. God always has His plan. It is up to you to find it.'

'I'm not sure I know where to begin,' said Ann.

'I once read a quote from a wise Buddhist woman. She said, "Before enlightenment – laundry. After enlightenment – laundry." When we first discover a profound truth it can seem as though life will never be the same. But when you look around you, you see that the world is filled with people of faith who are all muddling through, doing the best they can. None of us is perfect.

'We are in this world to live our lives as fully as we can, no matter how many mistakes we may make. This is not just a waiting room for Heaven. There is always laundry to be done, always work to be done. Take your time to make sense of this and what it means to you.

'Dry your eyes child. God did not enter into your life to cause you pain.'

Ann wiped her eyes and nose with the tissue.

'You have been so kind,' said Ann, 'thank you.'

'I hope that you will be just as kind to yourself and all those you love. That is my wish for you,' said the old woman. 'You, of all people must know how much you are loved. Carry that love with you always.'

And with that, the old woman stood, genuflected and left Ann alone to continue praying.

Chapter 24

'Okay', said Matt Feldman, 'this table looks solid, right? But really it's just a bunch of molecules and those molecules are made up of atoms. Those same atoms are made up of subatomic particles – which are not at all solid – really they're just information and energy. And that's true of every solid thing that you can see in this world. Same goes for our bodies. Everything that our eyes tell us is real is really just part of one huge energy field.

'The truth really is stranger than fiction. Everyone these days seems to think that science has all the answers – that there is just no mystery left in the world. I've loved science all my life. But I've got to tell you, it just kills me when I hear people using science as an argument against everything that is mysterious and spiritual.

'There are too many technicians out there who claim to be scientists, but they have no interest in asking any of the big questions when they don't already have the answers... So yes, science has its limitations, but it is also raises so many fascinating truths. Quantum physics would blow your mind. Heisenberg said that atoms are not things, they're only tendencies. Think about that. Think what that means. It means that everything you see – including this table – is a manifestation of consciousness.'

After a year of collecting stories from people around the country, Daniel's interviewing technique had matured. He knew it was always best to let those he interviewed vent their own particular ideas before he guided them gently back into giving a full account of their brush with death.

'So you were a scientist when you had your near-death experience?' asked Daniel.

The question brought Matt's attention back to the camera.

'I was the worst sort of scientist back then,' Matt said. 'I was the sort who thought I had all the answers. Sure, I had graduated top of my med school class only five years before, but I limited my vision and my thinking of the world to only what I could test and measure. There was no mystery in my life and no space for any mystery in the world. Science was more than just my career...my vocation, if you like. Science was my religion. And I was something of a young superman; saving lives and curing diseases. Back then I would probably have described myself as some sort of cellular robot. The arrogance of youth, huh?

'Of course the accident changed all that.' Matt paused, lost in his memories. 'I'd just pulled a 72-hour shift. Isn't it crazy how we expect physicians to function on so little sleep? We wouldn't trust a sleep-deprived pilot with our lives, but we'll let an exhausted surgeon or hospital doctor treat us. But that's the macho super-human environment of medicine for you.

'So I wasn't worried when I drove away from the hospital that night. It was something I'd done many times before. My thoughts, if I had any were of my bed. The journey was a simple twenty-minute drive that I'd made many times before.

'I was less than five minutes from my apartment when the crash happened. My first warning of danger, if you could call it a warning, was the noise of the initial impact. It was much later before I learned the details of what happened that night.

'The fact is, I don't know how long I was asleep at the wheel. My car was traveling at speed when I ran the stop sign at the intersection, and that's when I hit the side of Alice Denton's old Toyota. She died instantly. Her car was so badly crushed by the impact that I was told they weren't sure that there was anyone left in the car...

'The noise is something that I won't ever forget. It was just the most explosive mix of sound and shock and pain that you could ever imagine. There were just brief flashes of consciousness. I drifted in and out of all the noise and the pain for a while. Then there were some voices. When I woke, briefly, in the ER, I was surrounded by people and I could immediately sense their panic.

It turns out my aorta had been partially torn away from my heart. That's a common cause of death in patients who've been involved in high-speed car crashes. And it's surprisingly difficult to detect, so I was lucky they'd caught it in the ER. I needed immediate surgery to repair the rupture.

'I have no memory of being taken to the OR. The panic of the ER seemed to have just melted away into nothingness. So you can imagine how confused I was to find myself standing in the OR, looking at my attending and two of my fellow surgical residents as they worked.

'It was as if the accident had never happened. The pain had completely disappeared. I was confused. Had it all been a dream? And then I noticed that Charlotte, one of the surgical nurses, was crying. My attending noticed at the same time and ordered her out of the room. The bleeping of the monitors told me that the patient they were working on had crashed. Brad, the resident who was an old friend of mine, suddenly shouted, "Matt, you're not dying today... you're not dying."

'And that's when I realized that the body on the table was mine. And that I was dead. The monitors were going crazy, and I was that body on the table, but equally I was not. How could I be the body on the table when I was observing the entire scene? So I was evidently not my body. My body was not Matt Feldman, and it never had been, it had only ever been a vehicle for me.

'I understood that then as I watched the monitors and my dead body. There was nothing to worry about, because I wasn't actually dying, it was just my body. I was fine. Actually I was better than fine. I was happy. There was no pain...

'As doctors we're trained to view death as failure. And that had certainly been my thinking before the crash. Back then I didn't even have the good sense to view death as an inevitability; I viewed it as the enemy. At no point in my life had I ever thought to wonder, what happens when we die? Because like so many other things I was sure I already knew the answer to that question, and I simply saw death as the end. I absolutely believed that consciousness ended upon death. So to find myself experiencing my own consciousness when my body had clearly died was a profound moment for me. It changed my understanding of everything…

'I wanted to share this discovery with my colleagues. I tried to reassure everyone in the OR that I was fine. There was no need for such aggressive treatment, because I had already left my body. But of course they were unaware of my presence. And then, with no real warning, I was suddenly returned to my body. I don't remember anything else until I woke in the ICU three days later.'

'Did you share your experience with any of your colleagues when you woke?' asked Daniel.

'Only Brad,' said Matt. 'He thought I'd had some sort of drug-induced hallucination. Though he was slightly freaked when I told him I'd seen Charlotte ordered from the OR. He thought I must have heard the staff talking about that.

'I think I would have tried to explain my experience to more people if I hadn't been given the news that my driving had caused the death of Alice Denton… I'd built my entire identity on a commitment to saving lives, so finding out that my actions had caused the death of an innocent woman almost destroyed me. I struggled to understand why I had survived.

'It was a visit from the husband of Mrs Denton that gave me the strength to carry on. They'd been married for 40 years, you know. He came to visit me about a week after the accident. There was no trace of bitterness or anger in that man. He came to talk to me about Alice, and to tell me that she was a woman who believed in second chances.

'Since she wasn't around to tell me that I was forgiven, he thought it was his duty to do what she would have wanted. He didn't want his wife's legacy to be my destruction, when I clearly had such important work to do.

'I can't tell you how much that act of forgiveness meant to me...

'All in all I was a patient in my own workplace for almost six weeks. I had a lot of time to do a lot of thinking. And I certainly discovered what it meant to be a patient.

'When I finally returned to work, I was utterly transformed by everything that had happened to me. The survival of my consciousness, the transformative power of forgiveness and the barriers to healing that I had experienced as a hospital patient all combined to change my view of medicine. My understanding of what it meant to be a great doctor underwent a tremendous shift.

'For a time I considered leaving surgery, because it seemed to be more focussed on cutting than on patient care. But in the end, that's exactly why I stayed; because I figured that's where I could make the most difference.

'I no longer see my patients as I once saw myself – as cellular robots in need of repair. I am also aware that they have spiritual and emotional needs. And I make sure that they are treated in an environment that is most conducive to healing.

'Some years ago there was some well-documented research into the power of prayer. The effect on survival rates was undeniable. If the source of such an improvement had come from anything other than prayer, I can guarantee you that all of my colleagues would have implemented the research's findings. But of course, given the subject matter it was largely ignored by the medical community. But not by me. So now, before I start my day I make time to sit quietly in my office and pray for all of my patients. That's something that I would never have considered if I had not had my near-death experience.'

Daniel did not rush to fill the silence that followed that statement. He waited a moment before asking, 'Do you believe in life after death?'

Matt Feldman smiled broadly.

'Now that I know for sure that consciousness survives the

death of the body, I no longer see death as an end, but as a transition. I certainly have no fear of death.'

'And does religion now play any part in your life?' asked Daniel.

'In a way,' Matt replied, 'though I would probably describe myself as a spiritual man rather than a religious man. But yes, I do find a unique peace and connection in praying with a group of people. Going to temple is something that helps sustain me throughout the working week. It's another gift in my life that was only made possible through the crash and its aftermath.'

Psychiatric Discharge Summary

Date

Thursday, March 6th 2008

Doctor

Dr Conrad Mitchell

Patient Name

Ann Richards

Discharge summary

This discharge is at the patient's request.

Course in Hospital

The patient was an emergency admission to this psychiatric unit following an episode in St Patrick's Cathedral that her family physician believed to be manic or psychotic. She had absconded from the family home following an uncharacteristic exchange with her boss in which she had asked to be permitted to make a documentary on the subject of God and life after death (the patient is a renowned television journalist). After leaving her apartment, the patient went missing for over six hours. She was only located when the authorities contacted her place of work and informed them that she was refusing to leave a side-altar in St Patrick's Cathedral despite the fact that it was past closing time. A priest who went to her assistance reported that the patient was crying and claiming to be "at one with God".

Although the patient agreed to be admitted, she later admitted to feeling some coercion from her husband, Stephen, to do so.

A mental status examination and thorough medical testing determined that neither psychosis, mania nor any other Axis I, II or III disorders were present.

The analysis then dealt with the impact of the patient's recent near-death experience (and subsequent mystical experience in St Patrick's Cathedral) on her identity and object relations.

In November of last year Ann was a passenger in a near-fatal car crash on the Long Island Expressway. Her injuries were life-threatening. She claims to have had a NDE in which she was reunited with her deceased father and a stillborn sister (of whose identity she claimed to be unaware). An atheist before this event, Ann was deeply unsettled by her transient experience of a relationship to the divine, and of a profound sense of noesis.

This experience was in sharp conflict to the patient's former lifestyle, beliefs, and attitudes. All of her subsequent attempts to communicate the profound impact of her experience have been frustrated. Neither her husband nor her mother recognize her spiritual experience as legitimate.

The sudden and dramatic nature of Ann's NDE, coupled with her failure to make contact with a sympathetic listener and her poor physical health in the aftermath of the accident, led Ann towards a sense that her very identity was breaking down. The resulting radical shift in her personal reality was overwhelming and compounded by the pressure she felt from family members who wanted Ann to return to her old identity.

Although Ann never feared for her own sanity she was disturbed by her newfound sense of a higher control or power behind reality. She sought refuge in St Patrick's Cathedral in order to escape these pressures and to reconnect with the divine.

Her account of those hours spent in St Patrick's Cathedral indicate a mystical experience rather than a pathological problem. Her reported feelings of 'oneness', her sensing of profound 'truths', her absolute certainty of the importance of the experience and her sense of being overwhelmed by ecstasy are all indicative of a spiritual experience rather than a mental health crisis.

This experience has left Ann with a greater sense of meaning and purpose in her life. Many aspects of her functioning were either unchanged or improved in the aftermath of her NDE and subsequent mystical experience. Individuals in the midst of a tumultuous spiritual experience may appear to have a mental disorder if viewed out of context, but we now know that mental health's history of pathologizing intense spiritual crises has been unwarranted.

Sudden, radical changes in beliefs often disrupt the lives of the individual involved and those around them. The complications and disorientation that often accompanies such spiritual crises can be greatly exacerbated by unsympathetic physicians and family members.

Normalization of and education about the experience could play a crucial role in transforming the understanding of such events from bizarre or shameful to a stimulus for personal growth. Negative reactions can greatly intensify an individual's sense of isolation and block her efforts to assimilate the experience.

It is my recommendation that Ann should enter into a course of therapy where she is encouraged to explore the meaning of her spiritual experiences in greater depth. A course of couples' counseling might also lead her husband to a greater understanding of his wife's changed world view.

Final Diagnosis
Religious or Spiritual Problem (Code IV62.89)

Chapter 25

The virus spread far and wide.

At first Daniel had been able to keep some track of its progress. He measured, or at least he imagined that he measured its dispersion for a time, as best he could, through the emails he received and through the volume of traffic on his web site. His motives in even attempting to follow the progress of the benevolent virus that he had unleashed had been mixed.

He had felt affirmed by the mostly positive messages that he received and equally, in those early days, he had felt vindicated by the sheer volume of people who found both truth and value in the stories that he collected. He had watched as it had spread beyond the veteran community; surprised and delighted to connect with disparate and far-flung people all grappling with the same questions.

Even so, Daniel had thought the email was a joke.

There had been some press coverage of his work and it had been more favourable than he had hoped, but he did not seriously believe he had been invited to interview Ann Richards. In the end, he had demanded a phone number to ensure that his trip to New York was not a fool's errand.

When he had called, Ann Richards' voice had been unmistakable. It was quite a scoop to secure an interview with someone of her stature. Her participation would doubtlessly add credibility to all of the accounts featured on the web site. After a year of flying and driving around the country to record the near-death experiences of so many people, Daniel had finally found a solid level of confidence in his abilities as an interviewer.

However, the prospect of interviewing Ann Richards had caused him to lose some sleep. The woman was used to working in professional studios with full film crews and experienced journalists. He struggled not to feel foolish at the thought of arriving to see her alone, armed only with a camcorder and a notebook.

Still, he reminded himself, it was Ann Richards who had contacted him. She must have seen all of the information and interviews that he had posted online. There was obviously some compelling reason why she wanted to add her story to the others. He would treat her just like everyone else.

The first test of Daniel's decision to treat Ann Richards like all of the others who he had interviewed came as soon as she opened the door to him. There was something so uniquely odd and unsettling in coming face to face with the reality of a person whose image was intimately familiar to so many that Daniel found himself temporarily frozen. It was a reaction that Ann Richards had clearly become used to. She graciously welcomed him into her home; her warm reception gave him time to regain his composure.

He noticed that she was much smaller than he would have imagined. Her complexion was not nearly as flawless as it appeared on screen. Even so, she embodied the impossibly glamorous and wealthy elegance for which New York city women were famous. As she spoke he reminded himself of his mission.

'You must think this strange,' said Ann smiling.

'I appear to be in the business of strange,' said Daniel. 'But I was surprised to hear that you knew anything of my work.'

Ann took a seat and indicated that Daniel should also sit.

'Your work has helped many people,' said Ann. 'It has certainly helped me.'

'My intention... my hope was simply to share my story and the stories of some others like me so that it would offer some hope to people who had lost all sense of hope,' said Daniel. 'I wanted to use my experience to help to prevent suicides. But I appear to have stumbled on a much wider audience.'

'Life has a habit of ignoring our plans,' said Ann.

'Still,' said Daniel, 'I was surprised... I am surprised that you would choose to tell your story to me when there are obviously so many other options available to you.'

'There are always other options available to all of us,' said Ann. 'But if I have learned anything from the spiritual journey that I have been on in these last twelve months it's to trust my instincts.

'Situations and choices are never really good or bad, it's only our perception that makes them so. A lifetime of working in the media has given me a certain power, yes, that's true. But I choose to use that power to examine all of the options available to me. And your stories and your goal really resonated with me. I trust you not to distort the truth of my experience. And if, by telling my story on your platform I can contribute to somebody else's healing, then that is what I choose to do.'

She saw his surprise.

'I didn't always feel this way,' she said. 'When this first happened to me, I just wanted my old life back, and then I wanted everyone to share my point of view. It has taken me some time to arrive at the point where I can simply offer my experience without any expectation or fear. It has taken time to incorporate the truth of my experience into my life. I'm ready now to share that truth, whatever the consequences.'

'I prefer to begin filming as soon as possible,' said Daniel. 'Do you mind if I start filming now? Are you ready to begin?'

Ann nodded her agreement. She watched silently as Daniel set up his simple tripod, and when she began to speak she was clearly unfazed by the fact that she was now being recorded.

'I was travelling on the Long Island Express a year ago when my car was involved in a serious crash,' she began. 'I was a passenger in the rear of a limousine. Luckily I was wearing my seatbelt. My head was filled with work and deadlines, I wasn't paying any attention to the road – I was too busy working on a column. The first sign I had of trouble was the impact of the sports car that hit the rear of the limousine. I will never forget that sound of metal on metal…

'My car was sent into a huge spin. At that point everything felt like it was happening in slow motion. I remember screaming. It was such a total shock. But then I guess all accidents are unexpected. The car didn't even have a chance to stop spinning when we were impacted again by a second vehicle. At that point I had lost all sense of direction. We began to roll. We rolled over two, maybe three times. I was like an old rag doll in a tumble dryer. The situation was totally out of control, and I remember thinking that I would not survive…

'I passed out for a while. It was the ringing of my cell phone that woke me. At first I was conscious only of sounds; my phone was ringing, a car's horn was honking and I could hear country music somewhere off in the distance.

'The next thing that registered was the pain. Everything hurt. It even hurt to breathe… I tried to open my eyes, but there was too much blood. After that brief experience of consciousness I just passed out again.

'I don't remember leaving my body. But my next awareness was of standing outside the car and of surveying the entire scene. It didn't even occur to me to be concerned by this change of circumstance.

'I was too overwhelmed by an intense feeling of peace to wonder at how I had managed to escape the vehicle or how I had recovered from my injuries. Something deep within me knew that there was no need to worry. And I was, you know, so grateful to be free from pain.

'There was a woman in a pickup truck that had landed on its side behind my car. She was in bad shape. Her little dog had died and she was clearly in shock. I moved towards her to offer her some assistance, but she didn't seem to notice me.

'At that point I noticed the rescue workers who had gathered around my car. I wanted to reassure the fire crew and the rescue workers that there was no need to worry about me. And it was then, at that point, that I saw that they were working on my body.

'It sounds strange, I know, but I felt absolutely no connection to that body. I was completely and utterly at peace with everything, even when they said I was dead.

'In fact, hearing them say that I was dead somehow made sense of the growing feeling of ecstasy that I was experiencing. It was only then that I noticed the light that was shining behind me. As I turned to give my full attention to that light it became more and more beautiful. It was brighter than any light I could have ever imagined; yet it didn't hurt me to look at it. But it radiated so much more than light. The warmth that it delivered was accompanied by this feeling of complete love. And the more I concentrated on the light, and the closer I was drawn to the light, the more I felt myself to be filled by this feeling of perfect love.

'My awareness grew as I moved towards the light. There was an odd familiarity to everything that I was experiencing – as if a part of me had always known that this is what would happen. I was excited. I felt like I was going home. I also felt foolish that I had ever forgotten that I was loved so completely. I knew that I would join with the light. It was so obvious to me that we were all connected to that light and that we would all become one with the light. Again, I remember feeling slightly bewildered that I had forgotten such a fundamental fact of life.

'But before I could enter into the light, I was met by my father and another soul who I immediately recognized to be my sister Lauren, even though before the accident I had known nothing of this sister who had been stillborn before I was ever born. Our reunion was so exciting. My father knew how much I had missed him since his passing and he assured me that he had been watching over me. But he quickly announced that it was not my time. He responded to my disappointment by explaining that I still had work to do. He promised me we would all be together once more.'

Ann paused, smiling at the memory.

'After that, I don't remember anything until I woke up in the hospital five days later. The pain had returned with a vengeance and I remember feeling so disappointed and disjointed to be back in my body.'

'How did the experience change you?' asked Daniel.

Ann laughed.

'This happened a year ago. And here I am, talking to you, only now ready to share my experience with anyone who cares to hear it... Looking back it's as though I went through some of the steps that they say you go through when you are grieving – you know; denial, anger, acceptance? And that makes some sense to me, because I really did die to the life I had before.'

She paused for a moment.

'I have changed my career, lost some friends and I almost lost my marriage. So this newfound wisdom has come at a certain price. There have been some dark and difficult times. But through it all I have never doubted the truth of my experience.

'I now know that I am not my job, I am not my body and I am not my possessions.

'There is a tremendous liberation to be found in discovering that life is eternal and that we are all of us loved beyond our wildest imagination.

'When I look back on the person I was before my accident I almost want to weep... Whatever success I had was completely undermined by the fact that I was unconscious to the beauty of life around me. I identified myself completely with my goals, and those goals were never fulfilled. Nothing was ever really enough.

'In the course of my physical rehabilitation I would often walk on the beach outside our home in the Hamptons and also here, in Central Park. The bliss I found in those moments when I would still my mind to everything but the now was indescribable. And that opportunity had always been available to me, and is available to all of us, if we would only quiet our minds and appreciate each moment.

'I see the world with new eyes, and it's a much more beautiful place than I had ever imagined.'

'Would you describe yourself as a religious person?' asked Daniel.

'I would describe myself as a woman of faith,' said Ann. 'I know there is a God, or a creator or a universal power. The fact that I have come to this pretty late in life probably makes me a little more fluid in my appreciation of all faiths. I have explored the teachings of a number of religions in this last year and I have come to believe that they all express the same fundamental love for the same God. So I certainly do have a relationship with God, but it's not something that I could easily label. I don't have any religious agenda. When I pray now I keep it to a simple "thank you".'

Daniel turned off his camera.

'I hope my story will be of some use to you,' said Ann.

'You're sure about this?' said Daniel. 'You're sure you want to go public with your story?'

'You clearly don't read the tabloids,' said Ann.

Daniel shrugged.

'At some point in my career I became public property. Fame was never my goal, never my intention, but I guess when your face is broadcast into so many homes, for so many years, it's inevitable. People feel they know you. And when your life suddenly becomes news, as mine did after the accident, the public mood can quickly shift from concern to curiosity to the sort of twisted sense of entitlement that will feed on tabloid rumour and gossip.

'My silence created a vacuum that was filled by a wave of media speculation. A brief stint in a psychiatric unit, my resignation and a two-week separation from my husband created a feeding frenzy. I won't pretend that I wasn't scared, that it didn't hurt... It's taken all of this time for me to gain the strength to introduce the facts into all of the speculation and lies.'

'You're a brave woman,' said Daniel.

Ann paused.

'Some months ago, when I first had the idea of going public with my experience, I was warned that I would be committing professional suicide. And there may be some truth to that. But the funny thing is, it was my very youthful devotion to the power of the truth that attracted me to journalism in the first place. Somewhere along the line news reporting morphed into the business of spin; more concerned with image and demographics than having the courage to deliver stories that might challenge the audience.

'My experience falls outside the secular mainstream, I understand that, but that does not make it any less true. Even friends have mostly responded to my story in one of two ways – they either think I should have stayed a little longer in that psychiatric hospital or they think I've developed some sort of religious agenda.

'It's understandable, I suppose. Death is something that most people would rather not think about. Trusting in my experience could turn a person's sense of reality on its head. And I know more than anyone how unsettling that can be. I understand that difficultly well enough to remain married to someone who does not believe any of this. Months of marriage counselling did nothing to convince him of life after death. But I've learnt to accept that, to accept him as he is. Just as he has had to learn to accept me as I am.

'Are you married Daniel?' she asked him.

'I was divorced before any of this happened,' he replied. 'But it did take me a long time to talk about it. In fact, it took too long.'

'Nonsense,' said Ann. 'You're here now, aren't you? I have a feeling that we're all doing exactly what we're supposed to be doing. And these stories that you record and share online… even if they spark just a little hope in someone who really needs it, well, I can't imagine anything more important than that.

'I'm prepared for the consequences of all of this,' said Ann. 'I know I'm speaking the truth, and you know it too. Maybe whatever media frenzy comes out of this will actually help someone who really needs it. Besides, I can't keep news like this to myself.'

Daniel nodded in agreement.

'The Marine Corps taught me to never leave a man behind,' said Daniel. 'Right now there are plenty of Marines who get left behind. More of them are dying here than ever died out there in Iraq. They're dying of hopelessness and neglect.

'I've seen a lot of death and a lot of destruction. I can't say I see a world of beauty in quite the same way as you – but I do get glimpses. Doing this work gives me a sense of purpose that I've missed ever since I left the Corps.'

'So you're happy now?' asked Ann.

Daniel lips moved with the suggestion of a smile.

'You say "thank you" when you pray,' he said. 'Well I say "please let me serve", and that's what I try to do every day. I try to serve; I try to share the truth of my experience with people who really need a shot of hope. After all, how many people get to survive their own death?'

The world is like a ride in an amusement park. And when you choose to go on it you think it's real because that's how powerful our minds are. And the ride goes up and down and round and round. It has thrills and chills and it's very brightly coloured and it's very loud and it's fun, for a while. Some people have been on the ride for a long time and they begin to question: "Is this real, or is this just a ride?" And other people have remembered, and they come back to us, they say, "Hey, don't worry, don't be afraid, ever, because this is just a ride." And we kill those people.

Bill Hicks

Acknowledgements

This book owes its existence to the courage and generosity of everyone who has ever shared a personal account of a near-death experience. Having studied many hundreds of these accounts I have done my very best to accurately portray both the reality and the broad variety of these experiences. I owe a particular debt of gratitude to Leroy Kattein who was hugely generous in his support for my work. Likewise, Dr Pam Kircher, Dr Penny Sartori and Evelyn Elsaesser-Valarino all freely offered their expertise and kindly checked my manuscript for errors.

My depiction of war-torn Fallujah would not have been possible without the assistance of Chris Cataldo, a former Marine who served as an infantry rifleman in Fallujah. Another excellent source of information was the book, 'We Were One', by Patrick K. O'Donnell. There is always a risk in seeking to portray the experiences of warriors when a conflict is so fresh in our minds and yet so beyond the experience of most readers. I hope that all of those who serve in the military and their families will find some value in my attempt to bring the issue of post-traumatic stress disorder to a wide audience. Sadly, many veterans who suffer with PTSD remain a largely hidden casualty of war.

The work of Dr David Lukoff and the resources he has created to increase the spiritual competency of mental health professionals enabled me to create the fictional psychiatric report featured in this book. It is thanks to the pioneering work of Dr Lukoff and Professor Stanislav Grof that spiritual crises and near-death experiences are now unlikely to be pathologized.

Thanks also to Randy Hoyt for his assistance in providing an accurate translation of the Heraclitus quotation.

Death is a certainty that we all share, yet as a society we are strangely coy on the subject. It is my hope that this book will encourage conversation and thought on that most fundamental of questions; what happens when we die?

BOOKS

O is a symbol of the world, of oneness and unity. In different cultures it also means the "eye," symbolizing knowledge and insight. We aim to publish books that are accessible, constructive and that challenge accepted opinion, both that of academia and the "moral majority."

Our books are available in all good English language bookstores worldwide. If you don't see the book on the shelves ask the bookstore to order it for you, quoting the ISBN number and title. Alternatively you can order online (all major online retail sites carry our titles) or contact the distributor in the relevant country, listed on the copyright page.

See our website www.o-books.net for a full list of over 500 titles, growing by 100 a year.

And tune in to myspiritradio.com for our book review radio show, hosted by June-Elleni Laine, where you can listen to the authors discussing their books.

mySpiritRadio